Two birds, named *Jeeva* and *Ishwar*, having similar nature and always remaining together like friends, find shelter and live on the same tree. One among them eats and enjoys sweet fruits, i.e. assesses the results of the actions while the other does not. It just keeps seeing the other as a witness. In a similar way, ignorant *jeevatma*, though living with *Ishwar* (God) on the body-tree, is getting infatuated—by its helplessness and incapacity in achieving its desired results. But he sheds his sorrows and infatuation when he sees *Ishwar* and the complexities of His *Maya*, as he finds that *Yogis*, more brilliant and competent than him, have realized Him. What this statement means is that two birds, *Jeeva* and *Ishwar*, live on a tree known as the human body, and both of them have similar nature *Sat-chit-anand*. One of them, immersed in the *maya-moha* of worldly activities, undergoes joys and sorrows, whereas the other is constantly indifferent to all this and fixed in its own nature. When *jeevatma* becomes indifferent to the world, it is liberated.

Message of the Upnishads

Dr. B.B. Paliwal

DIAMOND BOOKS

ISBN : 81-288-1180-0

© Publisher

Published by	:	**Diamond Pocket Books Pvt. Ltd.**
		X-30, Okhla Industrial Area, Phase-II
		New Delhi-110020
Phone	:	011-41611861-65, 40712100
Fax	:	011-41611866
E-mail	:	sales@dpb.in
Website	:	www.dpb.in
Edition	:	**2014**
Printed by	:	Adarsh Printers, Shahdara, Delhi-110032

MESSAGE OF THE UPNISHADS
by : *Dr. B.B. Paliwal*

Contents

Foreword

Foreword

Upnishad is the name of spiritual knowledge or *Brahma-vidya*. They constitute the knowledge part of the *Vedas*. It is that eternally lit lamp of knowledge which has spread light since Creation. It is eternal, perennial and indestructible. Its light has that immortality which has nourished the roots of *Sanatan Dharma*. It is India's own treasure meant for the welfare of the whole world.

Up = near, *nishad* = *nishidati* = one who sits. *Upnishad* is that person who, having reached near the ultimate reality (*Param Tatva*), settles down quietly. The ultimate reality beggars description. The *Upnishads* lead us to the realization of that indescribable ultimate reality—*Parabrahma*. The *Upnishads* are the key to reach and unlock the ultimate reality.

There are 10 main *Upnishads*—*Ish, Ken, Katha, Prashna, Mundak, Mandukya, Taitiriya, Aitareya, Chhandogya* and *Brihadaranyak.*

Total *Vedas* are divided into 3 parts—the *Upnishad* part, the *mantra* part, and the *Brahman* part. The *Upnishad* part deals with the knowledge section (*Gyan-kand*) of the *Vedas*. In the present *manvantar* 1180 branches of the *Vedas* ensued. A similar number of the *Upnishads*, the *Brahman* and the *mantras* also followed. This count of the *Vedas* is obtained in the *Puranas* and the *Upnishads*. But today even a hundredth part of it is not available. *Granthas* equal to the *Upnishads* are found in the *Puranas* as well: for instance *Shrimad Bhagvad Geeta* in the *Mahabharata*, which is considered as the essence of the *Upnishads*. Seen in this context, we find that the bases of all of our religious *granthas* are in some form or the other at some place or another in the *Vedas*. Divorced from the *Vedas*, they have no existence at all.

Upnishad as a word has extensive meanings, the main being 'knowledge' (*Vidya*) and secondary a book. Since the *Upnishads* are the last part of the *Vedas*, they are described as the *Vidanta* as well. One of the joyous and appreciable traits of the *Upnishads* is their eagerness to find out the truth.

It is impossible to have the minute and subtle knowledge of Indian history and culture without understanding the *Upnishads*. There is hardly any evolved and developed Indian ideal the origin of which cannot be traced in the *Upnishads*. They are a perennial source of strength and creativity. It is only the *Upnishads* which can say, 'Take me from falsehood to truth, Take me from darkness to light, Take me from death to immortality!'

The *Upnishads* have their own design. They are an everlasting literature and for this reason we call them *Shruti*. We discover those truths which are beyond senses and mind bound by senses, which are beyond human comprehension and which can be realized only with the help of purified mind and rarified consciousness. The *Upnishads* are the perennial and universal truth and will always continue to inspire mankind. They call upon man to continuously struggle to attain the highest, the ultimate. They invite us to struggle to realize and experience in life the eternal, permanent *Amrit tatva*.

The *Upnishads* are an ideal instance of the tradition of teacher and disciple (*guru-shishya*). The deeper mysteries of Creation have been revealed in a very convenient manner, using the method of question and answer. Only the *Upnishads* could explain and elucidate *atma, parmatma, Brahma* etc. with the help of various illustrations, instances, metaphors, suggestions and logic. We could never have grasped the subtle meaning of the *Vedas* without the *Upnishads*.

In this book the treasure of knowledge, that the *Upnishads* are, has been presented in a simple style so that the common man could read and understand it and transform his life in its light.

—**Author**

The Upnishads: An Introduction

The *Upnishads* mainly deal with knowledge. Therefore, they contain a detailed description of knowledge related to the nature of *Brahma*, the relation between *Jeeva* and *Brahma* and the path leading to the realization of *Brahma*. Besides this, the deeper mysteries of the *Vedas* are also inherent in them. The origin of the word '*Upnishad*' is from the root '*sad*' with prefixes '*up*' and '*ni*' added to it. In clear terms, *Upnishad* is that knowledge which shows the path to reach and attain *Parabrahma*'.

The *Upnishads* are called mysterious *granthas* as well. Mysterious knowledge about the basic element has been a topic of discussion between the *guru* and his *shishya*. The *gurus* have been replying to the questions of their *shishyas* related to *tatva-gyan* and those questions and answers between the *shishya* and *guru* have been collected and compiled in these *granthas*. They are the last part of the *Vedas* and, therefore, they are called the *Vedanta* as well. Shankaracharya called them the symbol of *Brahma-vidya*. The *Upnishads* are definitely quoted from the *Vedic Samhitas* (collections). They are live and full of verve.

Literal Meaning

If the word '*Upnishad*' is analysed it means: '*Up*' i.e. near, '*ni*' i.e. with commitment, and '*shad*' i.e. to 'sit'. So it would literally mean, 'Sitting near a *guru* with commitment for *tatva-gyan* (knowledge of the basic element, truth).

The questions and answers exchanged between the *guru* and *shishya* were collected and thus *Upnishads* came into existence.

In ancient times the knowledge was not freely or readily made available to all and they remained a mystery. This is the reason they were termed as mysteries also. Like the *Brahmans* and the *Aranyakas*, the *Upnishads* too are related to different *samhitas*. The largest number of the *Upnishads* is related to *Krishna Yajur Veda*.

Period of Their Writing

It is absolutely impossible to separately determine the period of writing of individual *Upnishad*. According to Shri Radha-krishnan their period of writing can be assumed to be 6th century B.C. Philosophical thinking dominates ancient *Upnishads*. In later *Upnishads* the feelings of devotion and religion have found entry. Among the latest *Upnishads* one does not come across the depth and liberalism of the *Vedic Upnishads*. Most of them are not philosophical. They rather tend to be religious or devotional in nature, which propound the religious sects of a much later period.

The creation of the *Upnishads* is the result of thousands of centuries. According to Max Muller their period is 600 – 400 B.C. According to *Vedic Sahitya Parisheela*, a research work by Rajni Kant Shastri, the period of the writing of *Samhitas* is approximately 4533 B.C. If one studies the Christian thinking, it is presumed that the Creation came into existence between 5000 to 7000 years B.C. According to Indian thinking, the universe was created crores of years ago. From a scientific point of view also the creation of the world took place crores of years earlier.

Many scholars have undertaken research in order to determine the correct period of writing of the *Vedas* and the *Upnishads* but no definite or solid evidence is available in this regard.

The Number of the *Upnishads*

The number of the *Upnishads* is mentioned as 108 and at places as 200. The number, however, of the *Upnishads* which are important and acknowledged all around, is much less. In the following *shloka*, ten *Upnishads* counted, and they are considered important by common consent.

"*Ish-ken-katha-prashna-mundaka-mandukya-taittirih |
Aitriyashva chhandogyam brihadaranyakam tatha | |*"

So the 10 *Upnishads* are (1) *Ish* (2) *Ken* (3) *Katha* (4) *Prashna* (5) *Mundak* (6) *Mandukya* (7) *Aitreya* (8) *Taittiriya* (9) *Chhandogya* and (10) *Brihadaranyak*. Some persons count *Kaushitaki* and *Shwetashvatar* also among important *Upnishads*.

The Subject Matter of the *Upnishads*

The curious man has been busy with the questions—

'When? What? How? Why?'—right from the beginning. The *Upnishads* also describe the deep thinking related to these questions. When you read *Shvetashvatar Upnishad* you find that the *Brahma* knowing *Rishis* face these questions, which reflect the curiosities of that time right from the beginning. For instance, what is the basis of our life? Why are we alive? Is *Brahma* the cause of the whole world? etc. As per *Ken Upnishad* also, 'Who brings about *Pran* and who moves it? Who directs ad inspires us? Who tells our senses about their various activities?' As per *Kathopanishad*, *Brahma* is imbued with mutually contradictory traits, and he is the greatest— more subtle than an atom.

Paramatma (God) is present in the smallest as well as the biggest forms, and the purpose of life should be to understand and acknowledge the significance of the relation between *Vishvatma* (God) and *Jeevatma* (living being, man). The aim of the *Upnishad* is to impart the knowledge of *Brahma* to man and to understand the *tatva* (reality, element) of the soul. The reason is, if a man becomes *Brahma-gyani*, he forgets the game of birth and death. He remains lost in *Brahma* and attains salvation. On becoming a *Brahmagyani* a man understands the true nature of soul residing in his mortal body. *Atma* (soul) itself is *Brahma* and cannot be destroyed. It is *Ishwar* (God). When a man dies, his body is disintegrated and merges into five elements. But the soul merges in God and/or gets another body i.e. after leaving one body it acquires another.

In the context of self-knowledge, the *Upnishads* describe four states of man—The first one is of being awake. In this state a man performs various activities such as he exerts physically, eats, drinks, consumes things, feels joy, anger, happiness, suffering etc. It is an extrovert state.

The second state is the state of dreams in which man is involved in his desires. It is an introvert state.

The third state is one of sleep. In this state, man neither sees a dream, not has a desire, nor performs any actions i.e. he is always happy.

The fourth state is *turiya* in which all activities of man come to an end and he attains peace. All his dualism comes to an end, and he attains non-duality, and this non-dualism leads all living beings to see their soul element—brings them face to face with their soul. The *Upnishads* teach us the introvert *sadhana* (devotion, practice) and *Brahma-vidya* and how to attain it. *Parabrahma* is in *Brahma-vidya* and He is the cause of this Creation and He reveals, informs everything.

Meditation, knowledge, devotion – these are among many paths of *Sadhana* which have been described in the *Upnishads*. The men who traverse the path of *sadhana* automatically develop divine qualities in them. Truth has been stated as the base of *Brahma* in the *Upnishads*. *Om* is called the micro symbol of *Brahma*. Taking it as the best method of *Brahma-gyan*, the worship of *Om* (worship of *Pranav*) has been described. Different forms of *Parabrahma* have been described and explained in the *Upnishads*. The *Upnishads* describe the process through which *Brahma chetana* (divine consciousness) changes into *jeeva* (living being). How does He get His form? Which *ahutis* (offerings) are made for him to attain the form of *jeeva*?

Thus the deep, inner secrets of thinking and meditation of the *Rishis* have been described (in the *Upnishads*) which help man in standing face to face with *Parabrahma* and in gaining the knowledge of the truth.

Language and Style

Prose is generally the language of the *Upnishads*, though some of them are poetic as well. The subject is dwelt upon in the form of episodes and stories in prose form in the *Upnishads*. The *acharyas* have removed the doubts of their *shishyas* with the help of principles only. The dialogue between Yagyavalkya and his wife Maitreyi generates detachment to love for money and wealth in the hearts of men.

The deeper mysteries are thus conveyed with the help of philosophic scenes and episodes. They assume a very simple and natural form in the *Upnishads*.

Aim: Nearly all the trends of Indian philosophy are found in the *Upnishads*. But it we talk of the aim of the *Upnishads*, we find that they help men to attain the knowledge of the truth. They tend to answer questions arising in man's mind, they try to resolve doubts and problems in man's mind. Some perennial questions are asked, such as: What is *Brahma*? Who are we? What is the cycle of birth and death? Who is the master of the entire world—moving and non-moving?

So, it can be said that the *Upnishads* are a storehouse of knowledge, they act as a medium for the realization of *Brahma*.

The Importance of the *Upnishads*

If someone wants to know himself, then he should study the *Upnishads*: i.e. What is man? What is his *jeevatma*? How does *jeevatma* merge into *Paramatma*? A physician can tell you which organ or part of your body is where in it. What part does a particular organ perform in it? What is the temperature of your body? etc. But he will not be able to show your soul to you. What is your soul? What is *Brahma*? He may not be able to answer these questions. It is only the *Upnishads* which introduce a man to the fact as to what he is. We will not get this knowledge from any book of science. Another important issue and a matter of great secret is the fact that the truth cannot be described. Howsoever profound a scholar may be, he cannot describe the truth. The reason is that the truth can only be experienced. Take an example: We say that *gur* (crude sugar) is sweet. It is true that *gur* is always sweet, but a person, who has never tasted *gur*, would be at a loss to understand that *gur* is sweet. He will know this truth when he tastes *gur* i.e. the truth is the truth, whatever it is. But it can not be described. The truth can only be experienced.

Likewise what is *Brahma, Paramatma*? How can He be realized? It is true that a man can attain the knowledge of Brahma. He will tell others how to be a *Brahma-gyani*, because he has experienced the knowledge of *Brahma*. The other person, too, will accept it as *Brahma-gyan* only after he has experienced it. Likewise, imagine a man who has seen the immense form (*virat swaroop*) of God. Now this man, who has had this experience, who has had the *darshan* of God, cannot describe what *Ishwar* is, how he looks.

What I intend to say is this: the truth present in the *Upnishads* can be comprehended and experienced only on reading and studying them (the *Upnishads*). This in itself is sufficient to prove the depth, meaningfulness and significance of the *Upnishads.* They are replete with science and knowledge of endless variety. They help you experience the soul and God and the relationship between the two. They introduce you to the truth. However, the irony is that man treats his body as a means of enjoyment only.

We get this (human) body after crossing through 84 lakh forms of being, and unhappily we continue to indulge in evil deeds. There is only one reason of it. We do not know the truth. If a man wants to attain salvation, he will find the knowledge for it in the *Upnishads*. While describing human body, it has been stated in the *Upnishads* that it is covered under the layers of five *koshas*, and a man can attain salvation only after penetrating through them.

Panchkoshiya Human Body

The *panch* (five) *koshas* are present in human body in a micro and subtle form, and in this body itself the soul of man, which is a form (part) of *Paramatma* i.e. *Ishwar*, is also present. The *panch-koshas* of human body are:

(i) **Annamaya kosh**: When a child is born, then physical body is *annamaya kosh*. i.e. human body. It is related to body and for upto the age of 6-7 years it grows taking food and nourishment. Upto this age, it has no knowledge of the world as to what is affection, *maya*, suffering, happiness etc. It knows only hunger, appetite. It cries when it is hungry. Slowly and slowly this cover of a body reaches a stage where its (incremental) growth stops. This body needs food upto this stage starting from the beginning. If it does not get food, the body gets weakened, shortened and dying. This body is dependent on food only, and therefore, it does not have *Brahma* in it.

(ii) **Pranmaya kosh**: *Pran* means inhalation and exhalation of breath. This is a biological activity through which the wind enters the body, activates its parts, and helps directing some physical activities such as the flow of blood, digestion of food, and discharge of urine and faeces etc. It controls the temperature of the body also. Heart is its centre. This movement of the wind in the body helps us in speaking and pronouncing words.

When the wind enters the body, it transforms itself into five main and five secondary *pranas*. They are as under:

Pramukh (Primary) Pran

1. *Pran*: It is in the region of heart.
2. *Apan*: It is in the region of rectum.
3. *Udan*: It is in the region of throat.
4. *Vyan*: It is spread in the whole body.
5. *Saman*: It is in the region of throat in an equal form.

Gaun (Secondary) *Pran*

1. *Nag Vayu*: This wind is related to sneezing etc.
2. *Krikar Vayu*: This is related to hunger and thirst.
3. *Dhanajay Vayu*: This is related to the nourishment of body.
4. *Kurma Vayu*: This is related to constricting activities.
5. *Devdutt Vayu*: This wind is related to that activity of the body when a man feels sleepy, covers his eyes with eyelids and goes to sleep.

Pran Vayu keeps all the activities of the body going. This *Pran-Vayu* directs other activities related to *yoga* and enables the *yogis* to perform their *yoga sadhana*. This *Vayu* plays a significant role in the attainment of *Brahma*. But it is not *Brahma* in itself.

(iii) Manomaya kosh: This is the most important *kosh* of the body and helps it in realizing *Brahma*

Manomaya kosh is related to mind. Mind is generally in a state of flux. It moves fast. Its speed is never weakened. Brain is the central point of mind. All the activities of the body receive directions from it. In other words, it directs various activities of the body. For instance, which part has to do what? This is ordered by the mind. The activities of the body are dependent on the desires of mind. Mind controls and directs senses also. *Yoga* is possible with the help of this *kosh* and man can stand face to face with *Brahma* in realization. A *Brahma-gyani* is one who has controlled his mind.

(iv) Vigyanmaya kosh: This *kosh* is more subtle than the *Manomaya kosh*. Its centre is brain. It acts through intelligence, distinguishing things. Through intelligence we know the consequences etc. of a particular action. It inspires man to renounce *moha-maya* (affections and illusions). A *yogi* has to master (conquer) *Vigyan kosh* so that he may have the knowledge of *Brahma*. After mastering it, a *yogi* goes beyond intelligence and logic and moves ahead in his path towards *Brahma*. He develops faith in right kind of actions. That is why faith (*shraddha*) holds highest rank in *Vigyanmaya kosh*.

(v) Anandmaya kosh: *Anand* means happiness, full joy or bliss. A man attains and experiences *anand* only after he has realized *Brahma*. But happiness is happiness only. A person, lying dead inactive, rises up when he experiences joy. *Anandmaya kosh* is the seat (*sthan*) of *atma* and it is located in *brahma-randhra*, a place inside a man's skull. When a man attains or realizes *Brahma*, then that realization is not permanent, it is momentary. When a *yogi* knows his *atma* he realizes this *kosh* in a temporary manner. But if he wants to realize permanent joy or bliss, then he has to master *Anandmaya kosh* also. When a man, after identifying the truth, attains permanent bliss, he breaks himself free from *moha-maya* and the bondage of life and death. He attains *Para Brahma*. He attains salvation.

So a man becomes *Brahma-gyani* after having penetrated through these five *koshas*, and achieves salvation. Our *Rishis* did this for centuries and collected their experiences and the knowledge of truth in the *Upnishads*. They made other persons also see the truth. The *Upnishads* deal with this area of truth and experience, and tell us what *atma, paramatma* and *Brahma* are and how they are realized.

Atma, Paramatma

"*Samoaham sarvabhuteshu na me dveshyoasti na priyah |*
Ye bhajanti tu mam bhaktya mayi te teshu chapya ham | |"

According to this *shloka* of *Bhagwad Geeta*, "I do not feel jealous of anybody nor am I partisan to anyone. I have equi-balanced feelings for all living beings. But the living beings who serve Me with faith and devotion, they are dear to Me and dwell in Me, and I also love them and I am in them, too."

A jewel studded in the gold ring makes both itself and the ring beautiful. In the same way *Paramatma* and *Atma* (*jeeva*) are perennial lusture. *Paramatma* is the jewel and *jeeva* or *Atma* is the gold ring. So this is a continuous bond between *atma* and *paramatma*. The lure of *parmatma* is so strong that *atma* is always attracted towards attaining Him. It is not easy to realize God. It is the most severe *sadhana*. When a man attain the knowledge of *Brahma*, he is relieved of all bondages.

"*Yathaidhansi samidviagnirbhasmasatkurute Arjun |*
Gynagnih sarvakarmani bhasmasatkurute tatha | |"

According to this *shloka* of the *Bhagvad Geeta*, 'Just as the burning fire reduces the fuel to ashes, in the same way *agni* (fire) of knowledge burns down all the bondages of natural activities' i.e. here the mutual relation of God and soul is described by presenting a metaphor of fire representing comprehensive knowledge. This fire burns away the fruits of not only bad deeds but good deeds as well. *Prarabdha* and *beej* (seed) etc. are various forms of the fruits of action, but the knowledge of the form of *jeeva* (*atma*) burns away all of them and all the bondages of action of a man of perfect knowledge are burnt away.

"*Ubhe ubhaivaishete taratyamritah sadhavasadhuni*।"

According to this *shloka* from the *Vedas* a wise man is freed from the bondages of action (both good and bad). So the knowledge of God and the soul cannot be attained through proofs. It can be had from experience—personal experience only. Who is wise, the man of knowledge? The *Geeta* describes him thus:

"*Yada samharte chayam kurmodanganeer sarvashah*।
Indriyaninindriyarthe bhyastasya pragya pratishthata।।"

It means, just as a tortoise collects all the parts of its body into itself, in the same way the man, who takes his senses away from the objects of their desire, has a settled intelligence. This man in reality is *param gyani* (the most wise). Such a person is blessed by God, and attains Him.

"*Ragadveshaviyuktaistu vishayanindriyaishcharan*।
Atmavashyairnidhiyatma prasadamadhigachchhati।।"

According to this *shloka* of the *Geeta*, the person who, practising restraint, brings all his senses under control, receives all the blessings of God and thus he is freed from all affections and jealousies.

Lord Shri Krishna has called Himself the consciousness (*atma*) of *jeevas*, i.e. He is the Life force.

"*Vedanam Samvedoasmi devanamasmi vasavah*।
Indriyanam manashchasmi bhutanamasmi chetna।।"

"I am *Sam-veda* among the *Vedas*, Indra among gods, mind (*man*) among senses and *chetna* (soul) among *jeevas*. i.e. there is a difference between the soul element and inanimate nature. Inanimate nature does not have consciousness as is possessed by *jeevatma*. Consciousness is the highest and eternal, i.e. consciousness (*chetna*) can never be born out of the interaction of inanimate objects.

Likewise, there is an unbreakable relationship between *Jeevatma* and *Paramatma*, and man can realize it only through true knowledge. The reason is that *Paramatma* is present in our body in the form of *Atma* and He is the highest bliss as well as truth also.

What is the Truth?

When a man understands what is falsehood, or untruth, and smashes it, he knows the truth. Death is a reality. The day man realizes this truth, he becomes knowledgeable and wise. In the same way God is also a reality, ultimate reality. Therefore, the *Upnishads* are an easy and simple way to attain the knowledge of *Brahma*. They are a vast store of the knowledge of God, of the knowledge of the truth. But nobody can import you that knowledge. You will have to realize it yourself through experience, because *Brahma-gyani* is one who has realized or actualised the knowledge of *Brahma*.

What Do the *Upnishads*, According to the Scholars Say?

A number of scholars, both Indian and from abroad, have expressed their views in respect of the *Upnishads*. It would be relevant to present the views of some of them here:

Swami Vivekanand: "There is no discrimination in respect of caste, community, country, opinion etc. in the *Upnishads*. They ask every one: Rise and be self-reliant. A man should be independent spiritually, mentally and physically. The basic principle of the *Upnishads* demonstrates this. Whenever I studied the *Upnishads* tears rolled out of my eyes wondering how great is this knowledge. With what severe devotion this knowledge was collected in the *Upnishads* ? We can draw strength and energy for a new life from the *Upnishads*."

Rabindranath Tagore: "The sunrise has started lighting the east with its rays. When it comes to the middle of the sky at noon, it will light up the entire globe and every one will be able to see that this *Brahma-gyan* is the religion of the whole world."

Acharya Vinboba Bhave: "I have accorded *Bhagvad Geeta* the status of mother in my life. But about *Upnishads*, I will say that they are the mother of my mother."

Dara Shikoh: "Among the Hindu books of knowledge of God, the *Upnishads* are a vast store of spiritual joy and peace. I studied *Quran* and many other works related to Islam i.e. religion. But all the description in them about God could not quench the thirst of my heart."

Acharya Shriram Sharma: "The *Upnishads* contain that subtle, deep and mysterious knowledge which you get only on realizing your soul."

Pandit Ravi Shankar Shukla: "The *Upnishads* have been an invaluable treasure of our Indian culture for ages."

Govind Vallabh Pant: "The *Upnishads* are the original springs of *Sanatan* philosophical knowledge. They are not only the result of brilliant intellectual skills, but they are the result or fruits of experience of ancient Indian *Rishis*."

Max Mueller: "I am indebted to the *Upnishads* because their studies have played an important role in my progress. They are and will remain venerable in the world in advancing spiritual knowledge through spiritual knowledge when compared with other literature. They are that encyclopaedia of knowledge which frees man from fear of death."

Baver: Indian *Upnishads* are that invaluable treasure of the world literature related to the knowledge of God, which provide real spiritual solace and peace."

Paul Dyson: "The philosophical postulates of the *Upnishads* are rare not only in India but in the whole world."

Schaupenheur: "There is no other scripture in the world equal to the *Upnishads* in terms of advancement and welfare of human life."

Baldev Upadhyay: "The *Upnishads* are the main source of the *tatva-gyan* (knowledge of the ultimate truth) and principles of religion. They are that reservoir from which innumerable rivers of knowledge originate and irrigate all around with knowledge. The *Geeta* and the *Brahma-sutra* are dependent on them."

Seen thus, the knowledge contained in the *Upnishads* is a vast store for India but for the welfare of all humanity around the world.

The Upnishads Related to Rig Veda

The main *Upnishads* related to the *Rig Veda* are ten. They are:

1. *Aitreya Upnishad*
2. *Mudgal Upnishad*
3. *Nadbindu Upnishad*
4. *Kaushitaki Brahman Upnishad*
5. *Akshamalika Upnishad*
6. *Brihavricha Upnishad*
7. *Saubhagyalakshmi Upnishad*
8. *Radha Upnishad*
9. *Nirvana Upnishad*
10. *Atmabodh Upnishad*

What is the message of the *Upnishads*? Let us look into them and study in a proper order:

(1) Aitreya Upnishad

This *Upnishad* has three chapters. Its fourth, fifth and sixth chapters have chiefly the description of the knowledge of Brahma as their subject matter, and this is the main reason to entitle it as *Upnishad*. It is as follows:

First Chapter: This chapter has three sections dealing with and describing Creation, origin of the food grains, and the way the soul enters human body. The following are its three sections.

First Section: This section describes the origin of this universe, its creation. According to it, "The soul was in the form of a flame (of light) in the beginning of creation. The work on the beginning of creation started with an idea. The soul entertained the idea of creating *Lok* (world) and *Lok Pal* (Governor/Administrator). And then the soul (God/ *Parameshwar*) began the work of creation. First of all four *Lokas* were created: *Ambha, Marichi, Mar* and *Aapah Mahah, Janah, Tapah, Satya* and *Dyulok*—All these *lokas* are above *swarg* (heaven) and are known as *Ambha*. *Marichi* is the name of a *lok* which is lit up, i.e. it is space where the sun, the moon and the stars shine. It is called *Dyulok* as well. *Mar* is that *lok* where man comes and goes, i.e. where he takes his birth and dies This is *mrityu lok*. All the objects in this *lok* are ephemeral i.e. subject to decay and destruction. That is way it is termed as *Mar*, *Mrityu-lok* or *Prithvi-lok* (the earth). The fourth is *Aapah-lok*. This *lok* is below the earth, i.e. *Patal lok*. *Aapah* is called water also. Thus they are the four *lokas*. But the expression used is '*tri-lok*'. The reason is that *Ambha* and *Marichi* both are in space. So they are treated as one. *Prithvi* and *Patal* are two *lokas*. So the three *lokas* of *Trilok* are space (*Antariksh*), *Patal* and *Prithvi*.

Parameshwar (God) created the *lokas* in the manner. After creating them, *Ishwar* (God) started the work of creating *Lok-Pals*. *Aapah* i.e. water is treated as the most active in the *Rig Veda*. *Parameshwar* himself took birth from water in the form of *Hiranyamaya purush*. This is known an *Hiranyagarbha* as well. From this watery embargo God created *Hiranya purush*. From this *Hiranyagarbha*, which was in the form of an egg, the first hole of mouth was created. From mouth, *Vak* or *vani* (sound) i.e. the sense dealing with sound was created. From this was created fire, then the nostrils of the nose, and *pran* and from *pran*, *vayu* (wind) was created. Then after that the two holes of eyes appeared. From them (the holes) *chakshu* or the faculty of seeing was born. *Suryadev* (the Sun) was born from them. After that the holes of both the ears, or the sense of hearing, were born, and from them the sustainers/nourishers of the *dishas* (directions), i.e. *dik-pals* were created.

After that skin, and from it cells, and from cells medicines in the form of vegelation were created. Heart was born after that. From it came *man* and its presiding deity, the moon, was created. Next came the navel. From it originated *apan-vayu* (the wind which is not used), and from it came death. At the end of all, penis, the sense organ that creates life, was born. semen was born out of it. From semen, *aapah* i.e. the god of water was born. Water is creative, semen is that seed which creates more seeds for creation.

So, this section describes how the creation originated, and how this process of development forged ahead.

Second Section: This section describes the origin of human body. All the gods created by *Parameshwar* came into this ocean of the world. They felt hunger. They prayed for food grains and for a body which could eat these food grains, and for a body which could eat these food grains. *Paramatma* gave those gods the bodies of cow and horse, but they did not accept those bodies. Then God showed them human body. Various gods felt happy on seeing that body. Fire entered into human mouth and occupied the place of sound, *vani*. Through the holes of nostrils, *Vayu dev* occupied his place and was known as *pran-vayu* (life-giving wind), *Surya dev* occupied his place in the eyes. The *Dik-Pals* occupied their place in both the ears. The moon occupied his place in the heart, the seat of *man*. Death occupied its place in human body, entering through the rectum in the form of *apan-vayu*. The god of water found its place in the penis in the form of semen. In this way, all the gods occupied their respective places in human body, Hunger and thirst also asked from some place for themselves. God gave them some portion out of *havi* (offerings to god in the *yajna*) for gods. In other words they were given some place by way of share out of the food for gods. Seen thus, hunger and thirst do not have any independent place for them. They are connected with the powers of gods.

So human body was created in this manner, and all gods have their respective places in it.

Third Section: This third and the final section of the first chapter is about the origin of food grains and the path of entry through which soul entered into human body.

The decision to create food grains for the satisfaction of hunger and thirst of gods, after they had been allocated their respective places in human body, was taken. For this the *panch-mahabhutas* (five basic elements)—the earth, water, fire, wind and the sky—were baked (heated) to bring food grains into existence. When the food grains were ready and God asked it to be taken, then *vani* in the form of human body could not take it. If that was possible, then *vani* would have satisfied itself just with a description of it. The nose could also not take it, because in that case it would have satisfied itself just by smelling it. The eyes, ears, skin, hand and penis could also not take it, because in that even they would have satisfied themselves just by seeing, hearing, touching or experiencing it. Therefore, *pan* i.e. (the door of) mouth succeeded in taking it in. Since then mouth has been taking it in and it is maintaining and protecting human body with its intake of food grains.

Thus, after completing the job of creation of human body and food grains, *Paramatma* thought of the kind of relationship he would have with this human body: "Some part of Me should go into it". Then *Paramatma* found the hard part of man's head as a suitable place for Himself and entered it. As soon as He entered human body, all the gods present there came into a state of awareness, became conscious. The upper part of the newly born baby is the most tender, and from here *Paramatma* entered it. This is known as the spot of *Brahma-randhra* in human body. Piercing through it, God entered human body via this route. This spot is the gateway to the realization of *anand* (happiness). God has three spots where He rests and resides—heart, *Brahma-dham* and *Brahmanda*. He has three dreams also. The *purush* who appeared from human form, seeing the five elements (*panch bhut*) asked, "who is the other one here?" He found there only *Para-Brahma*. He was happy on seeing Him i.e. the *jeeva* born in human body saw Para-Brahma *Paramatma* in His subtle form; *man* saw Him face to face, realized Him and said, "*Indra*," which means "I saw Him, i.e. I realized Him (*Paramatma*)." That *Paramatma* is famous by the name of Indra, and in an indirect way God (*Paramatma*) was called Indra, i.e. (He) is one who cannot be seen with eyes, but can be experienced through heart.

Therefore, this can categorically be stated that this human body is the abode of *Paramatma*. He resides in *Brahma-randhra*, which is located in human skull. The *yogis* (aspirants) undertake strict *yoga sadhana* to reach Him, to realize Him. A *yogi*, who on completion of his *sadhana* reaches this place, he realizes God and is designated as *Brahma-gyani.*

Second Chapter: It has only one part. It describes what three births of man are. They are as under:

The glow or brilliance showing itself in all parts of human body is semen, which resides in human body and which through a process of ploughing and irrigation is placed in the womb of a woman. She nurtures it, and upto the time of the birth of the baby she takes its care as of herself. When the baby comes into this *lok* (world) from the body of his mother, i.e. when he is born, it is called the second birth of man. Now this infant grows gradually and becomes big and performs his duties. In this way, he performs his duties as a representative of his father, and finally on growing old, he dies. When he dies, it is his third birth.

Rishi Vamdev, too, has clarified this position. "When I was in the womb, I had understood the mystery of the birth of gods. Before gaining this knowledge, I was shackled in a strong cage." Strong cage refers to births in various forms of being. Vamdev understood the cycles of birth and death through realistic knowledge, and he gained fundamental knowledge (*tatve-gyan*) that 'now I am free'. In this way *Rishi* Vamdev attained *tatva-gyan* and, on being immortal, realized the happiness of heaven.

Third Chapter: In this chapter of the *Upnishad* we find as to what is the form or description of that God (of man) who is to be worshipped. What is that *atma* or soul that enables us to hear, see, smell and speak? It is as follows:

It is man's soul (*atma*) which helps him see and realize *man*, knowledge, science, *pragya* (unique capacities of knowing), *midha* (strong intelligence), *avesh* (flush of feelings), *vivek* (sense of discrimination), *Veg* (force), *pran shakti* (life force) etc. It enables man to realize the powers of *Paramatma*. Therefore, it is the soul. In all the three worlds (*trilok*) all—i.e. gods like *Brahma* and Indra, living beings born of five elements, and *andaj* (i.e. born from an egg), *svedaj* (born from sweat), and *udbhij* (born from an embryo), elephants, horses, cows etc. act according to the will and nature of God. He sustains all *lokas*, i.e. *Paramatma* is Himself *Brahma*; one who realizes Him becomes immortal an reaching *svarga-lok*.

(2) *Mudgal Upnishad*

This *Upnishad* of the *Rig Veda* has four sections. This *Upnishad* of the *Rig Veda* deals solely with one *suktas*. It describes the *virat swaroop* (limitless form) of Lord Shri Hari (Vishnu), the origin of men, *lokas* and *jeeva*. The sections are as under:

First Section: There is the *purush sukta* in this section. Lord Vishnu has been described in detail as follows:

Shri Vishnu has been called *Sahasra Sheeshi*. *Sahasra Sheeshi* means one who has a thousand heads. Another word used is '*dashangulam*' which means that Lord Shri Vishnu is placed 10 finger-width above this world. Shri Vishnu is said to have existed in all periods. He provides salvation. He grants salvation to all the persons engaged in good deeds. The form (appearance) of Vishnu is said to be related to *chuturvyuha* (four labyrinths) i.e. He is *chaturvyuhi*. It is stated that the whole universe originated from Him. There is a description of origin of nature and *purush* (man) from *Narayana*. This is alongside of the description of creation of the universe. One who gets the knowledge of this *purush sukta* is liberated, i.e. he attains salvation.

Thus, Shri Hari (Vishnu) is called the creator as well as the provider of salvation of creation in this section. He is the owner and sustainer of the entire universe—*charachar*, i.e. moving and fixed.

Second Section: In this section Lord Vasudev exhorts Indra, who has sought his shelter, to understand the subtle element. It is stated that *Purush* (God), who is beyond names and appearances, is beyond comprehension of anyone in this universe. Therefore, that inaccessible God has been described here in endless artistic forms for the welfare of gods and men. One can attain salvation only on having His *darshan*. *Trikalatmak Narayan* (God, existing in the past, the present and the future) exists in *purush* form. He is the best among all the glorious persons, and liberates all living beings. Shri Vishnu, transforming Himself into *Chaturvidha*, is present in the sky in His three steps and from His fourth step, known as *Aniruddha Narayan*, this universe is created. In his fourth step in the course of creation, He first created Nature (*Prakriti*). But when Brahma, embodied and in the form of Nature (*Prakriti*) could not understand the activities of creation, then *Aniruddha Narayan* exhorted him, saying, "O *Brahmadev*! Imagining yourself as a performer of *yajna*, and thinking of senses, take your body, born out of *kamal-kosh* (lotus stem) as *havi*, Me as fire, the spring season as ghee, the summer season as *samidha* (wood pieces used in the yagna) and *sharad* (season) as *rasa* (joy, ripened fruit). Then your body will become strong as *vajra* (stone) and then you will be able to see this Nature (*Prakriti*), *jeeva* and universe (*Jagat*)."

It is also described here that when *jeeva* meets its soul, i.e. when a *yogi* understands his soul with the help of his yoga, then this meeting of *jeeva* with soul grants him salvation. In other words on his recognition of soul and *brahma*, *jeeva* becomes *tatva-gyani* (knower of the ultimate reality) and after that on reaching his full, mature age, he attains salvation.

Third Section: In this section are described the worship in various forms of *purush* (Shri Vishnu) by different aspirants in their various forms of being i.e. it is one God who, by entering into many, assumes different forms. God manifests Himself in different forms by infusing His partial glow and vitality into them. He is worshipped in different forms. For instance, he is recognized as *Urdhvayu* in the form of *agni* (fire) and the performers of *yajna*, following the *Yajurveda*, recognize Him as *yajush* and perform *yajnas* for Him. The singers of *Sam* recognize him as *Sam*. This universe is inherent in Him. Worshippers such as snake, *sarpavida*, deity, nymphs, devotees and *Pitars* recognize and accept Him as poison, *pran*, *amrit* (nectar), *Gandhana*, deity and *Swadha*.

In other words, people worship Him according to their own feelings and inclination. Gods call Him *amrit*. The *Brahma gyanis* call Him *Brahma*, "*Aham Brahmasmi*", i.e. 'I am Brahma *Paramatma* also looks upon His aspirant devotees with a feeling of consideration and adjusts Himself according to them. In other words, God is realized by the people in the form in which they like and see Him.

Fourth Section: This section of the *Upnishad* describes the uniqueness and various constituents/ingredients of the above mentioned *Purush* when He appears. Additionally, this mystery is also revealed as to how this superior knowledge should be passed on to others.

Brahma is stated to be beyond three *tapas*, six *koshas*, six *urmies*, six *vicars*, six enemies, five *koshas*, and six illusions which are as under:

(1) Three *tapas* (fevers): of body, of the physical world, and those given by gods.

(2) Six *Koshas*: skin, flesh, nerves, blood, bones and marrow.

(3) Six *Urmies* (waves): hunger, sorrow, affection, thirst, old age and death.

(4) Six *Vikars* (Weaknesses/defects): dearness, bitterness, growth, change, jealousy and destruction.

(5) Six *enemies*: lust, anger, greed, arrogance, affection and *matsarya* (rivalry).

(6) Five *Koshas*: *Pran, Man*, food grains, joy and *vijnan*.

(7) Six illusions: family, *Gotra*, caste, *varna, ashram* and *roop* (good looks).

When *Param Purush* (God) assumes all these characteristics,

He becomes *jeeva*.

One who studies this *Upnishad* daily becomes pure, is elevated and refined.

The *Purush-sukta* of this *Upnishad* is a great secret and full of mysterious meanings. The method of its exhortation is like this: The scholar *guru* should sit on a clean and pure place; he should in *Pushya nakshatra* think of God while practising *pranayam* and observing highest discretion speak it slowly into the right ear of his disciple. The *guru* should not talk too much, because that fouls the message. This should always, and again and again, be spoken into the ear. Thus, both the exhorting *guru* and the receiving disciple attain the status of *Purna Purush* (God) in this life itself.

(3) *Nadbindu Upnishad*

In this *Upnishad* of the *Rig Veda*, the form/nature of *Omkar* (*Om*) has been described as a swan. Additionally, the twelve *matras* (sound arrangements) are described in a way that life should end gloriously in one of them. Subsequently, it describes how *man* (mind) should be controlled or brought into harmony with the help of *nad* (sound). It has three sections.

First Chapter: 'Om' has been described here as a swan. This description is found in the first section.

First Section: In Aum (*Om*) 'a' is the right wing, 'u' is its left wing, 'm' is its tail. The *ardha-matra* is the head or the top part of *Aum*. Both the legs of the swan are *Rajogun* and *Tamogun* and its body is *Satogun*. *Bhuh, Bhuwah, Swah* and *Mah lokas* are placed in its legs, thighs, back and navel, *Janalok* (the common man's world), *Tapolok* (the world of the ascetic), and *Satyalok* (the world of truth) are in its heart, throat and eyebrows. Its right eye is *dharma* (righteousness) and the left *adharma* (wrongdoing).

A devotee who, riding on the swan of '*Omkar*', performs *yajnas* or *anushthans* in a proper way, is not only rid of his sins, he attains salvation also.

Second Section: In this section of the first chapter, the 12 *matras* (sound connotation), and their nature are described like this:

The first *matra* is *agneyi* (fire), the second *Vayavya* (wind), the third is *Makar* and the fourth is *ardha-matra* (*Varuni*). All these four have three *mukhas* (periods) each. Taken all together, they are 12 *Kalas* (individual forms/strengths). That is why *Omkar* is described as having 12 *Kalas* (strengths). These twelve kalas are like this:

"*Ghoshini, Vidyunmala, Patangi, Vayuvegini, Namdheya, Aindri|*
Vaishnavi, Shankari, Mahatti, Namdhuti, Nari evam Brahmi| |"

These twelve *kalas* are known by these names.

The effect of these 12 different *kalas* (*matras*) is felt differently by men, depending upon as to in which *kala* he is ending his life. In other words, a man, in his next life, is born according to the *kala* in which he laid down his previous life.

"*Pahalayam tu matrayam yadi pranairviyujyate|*
Bharatvarsharajasau sarvabhanmah prajayate| |"

According to this 12th verse of the first chapter of this *Upnishad*, "If a person ends his life in the first *matra* then he can be the omnipotent emperor of *Bharatvarsha* in his next birth." Likewise, other *matras* too have their effect. For instance, one dying in the second *matra* is born as famous *Yaksha*, one dying in the third *matra* is born as a scholar, one dying in the fourth *matra* is born as *Gandharva*, one dying in the fifth *matra* is born with the spleandour of gods, one dying in the sixth *matra* is born as equivalent to Indra, one dying in the seventh *matra* reaches close to Lord Vishnu, one dying in the eighth *matra* attains proximity to *Rudra*, one dying in the ninth *matra* is reborn in *mahlok* (the region of joy), one dying in the tenth *matra* is born in *Janalok*, one dying in the eleventh is born in *Tapolok* and one dying in the 12th *matra* attains perennial *Brahmalok*.

Third Section: How a man can have the feeling of *Brahma* through meditation is described in this section.

All kinds of enlightenment emanate from the knowledge of *Brahma*, and a *yogi*, through a control of his *senses*, slowly and slowly leaves all the temptation, and finally gives up his ego as well. Thus, that *Yogi*, free from all bondages, attains salvation, stands face to face with *Para-Brahma* and enjoys bliss. Therefore, one should ceaselessly strive for self-knowledge, one should not feel excessively worried about the results of the deeds performed in the previous births.

The *prarabdha* (accumulated effects of actions of previous births) does not go away even after the attainment of self-knowledge. When a man see a dream in his sleep, he realizes its illusory nature only after waking up. In a similar manner the illusory nature of *prarabdha* dream is realized after self-knowledge.

The accumulated actions of the past lives are called *prarabdha*. A man with self-knowledge considers the previous births and lives as illusion. So, what is *prarabdha*? For a man gifted with self-knowledge, this body is also like a mere indication of dream. Just as soil is the base of all earthen vessels, likewise the soul is the cause of the entire jangled and tangled world.

According to the *Vedanta*, ignorance is the root of all these things. With the disappearance of ignorance, this world also disappears. In other words, for an enlightened person the world is not the world. He treats it as an illusion in which rope appears to be a snake. When you know, discover the rope, you give up all illusions.

Likewise worldly doubts disappear when one attains self-knowledge. When an aspirant attains this stage, then he does not see his *prarabdha*. It is only an ignorant man who is enmeshed in the issues of *prarabdha* etc.

Second Chapter: Sounds of *nad* are separately described in this chapter. An aspirant, as he advances on his path of devotion, hears these sounds.

When one starts *yoga-sadhana* he hears the sounds of *nad* in a loud form. Once he slowly moves ahead on his path of devotion he hears the sound of *nad* in a receding order, say as that of the ocean, clouds, bugle, waterfall, then that of the musical instruments, and finally as the sound of jingle bells, flute, violin and the humming of the bumblebee. This is called *nad anusandhan* (research of sound). An aspirant should get lost in a *nad* in which his heart finds rhythm and harmony.

Third Chapter: This chapter deals with the controlling of heart through *nad* or putting in into harmony. A *yogi* reaches the state of *turiya* or enlightenment in this way.

One should harmonise one's heart according to *nad* and immerse in it.

"Sarvachinta samutsrijya sarvacheshtavivarjitah
Nadmevanusandadhyannade chittam viliyate."

According to this *shloka*—

"A *Yogi* abjuring all his worries, and keeping his concentrated or indifferent search for that *nad* which interests him—i.e. he should seek harmony. Just as a bumblebee only sucks the juice of a flower, and does not smell its scent, likewise an aspirant finds bliss in *nad* and not in its object. A man, having a venomous nature like that of a snake, too, forgets worldliness."

When *nad* is combined with *pranav* (*Omkar*) it partakes the character of light, and is immersed in it. This is the highest state in devotion of Shri Vishnu.

A man's mind thinks of the sky as long as he hears the *nad*, or sound. If the *nad* slows down, heart, too, waves and meanders.

When the letter disappears from *nad*, then this is the highest state. Pursuit of *nad*, immerse the mind in *Para Brahma*, destroying all passions.

In a state devoid of mind, the body becomes dead like wood. It does not experience heat or cold, nor happiness or pain, neither respect nor dishonour. A *Yogi* is freed from dreams, sleep and wakefulness. His mind is calmed and settled and it attains the stage of enlightenment.

(4) *Kaushitaki Brahman Upnishad*

This *Upnishad* begins with this recitation for peace:

"O God! May my voice rest in mind, may my mind rest in my voice. You appear before me. Grant me the knowledge of the *Vedas*. Let me not forget what I have learnt through hearing. Let me devote all my energies to this study. Let me speak the truth. Protect me. Protect my *Guru* also. Protect both of us. May all the three kinds of pains—caused by body, gods and the world—calm down."

This *Upnishad* of the *Rig Veda* has four chapters. Different forms of worship are described in these chapters, such as the worship of *pran* (Life), *Agnihotra* (*yajna*) and, additionally, the worship of the element of consciousness. It details out the definition of *Brahma* and the knowledge of *Brahma*. These chapters are as:

First Chapter: This chapter describes *agnihotra* and its relationship in respect to the knowledge of *Brahma*.

Maharshi Chitra, the grandson of Rishi Garg, invited Maharshi Udyalak, the son of Arun, for *yajna*. But he could not come for this purpose. He sent his son, *shwetketu*, for participation in and completion of the *yajna*. On reaching there, *Shwetketu* sat on a high, elevated seat. Maharshi Chitra asked, "Is there any elevated place in this world where you would like to place me? Or would you place me at a place which is shrouded in a wonderful cover?" On hearing this, Shwetketu said, "I have no knowledge in this field. I will get an answer to this question from my father." Having said this, he came back to his father, and asked him to answer this question. Udyalak Rishi said, "Son! I too do not have an answer to this question. Come on, let us go to the *yajnashala* of Maharshi Chitra for an answer."

Carrying *samidha* (wood for *yajna*) in his hands, *Udyalok*, along with his son came to Maharshi Chitra and said, "O Maharshi! We have come to you for divine knowledge. Kindly oblige us." Then Maharshi Chitra said to them "O *Munivar!* You are the best among Brahmins, and yet you have come here. I will pass on to you knowledge in reality. You are entitled to it. Those who perform noble deeds in their lives attain and reach heaven after leaving this world. But the people who crave for *Chandralok* or heaven for the sake of pleasure and happiness lose all their pious deeds, and they fall back on this earth again i.e. they are reborn here and do not attain salvation. They are born in one of the forms of beings such as gnat, insect, tiger, lion, fish, dog etc." Then soaking in what the heaven and hell are, Udyalok asked, "*Munivar!* Who am I? How can I free myself from the bondages of this world?"

On hearing this, Maharshi Chitra exhorted him the knowledge of *Brahma* and said, "*Brahman!* The noble soul reaches the other world through two paths—*Devayan* and *Pitrayan*. When the soul reaches the other world through *Devayan*, then it attains salvation and is not reborn. But through *Pitrayan* the soul is re-born, and enters into one of the forms of being.

Taking the *Devayan* path, the soul traverses through *Agnilok* (the sphere of fire), then *Vayulok* (the sphere of the winds), *Varunlok* (water), *Adityalok* (the sphere of the sun), then *Indralok* (abode of gods), *Prajapatilok* and then finally *Brahmalok*.

At the entry gate of *Brahmalok* there is a pond of water, named '*Aar*'. Lust and anger rule this pond. If one is engulfed in it, he loses all his pious deeds. One has to use one's discretion to save oneself from this. After that there he meets a god, named *Yeshtiha*. Then there is the *Viraja* river. On seeing this river he loses his physical fatigue. Then there is a tree named *Ilya*. Beyond that there is a place more beautiful than that of Indra and *Prajapati*. Two watchmen of Brahma live in this palace. It has an assembly hall named *Vibhupramati*. The altar is named *Vichakshana* and *Amitauj* the *asana* of Brahma. It is called *Paryak* as well. *Manasi* is his wife. *Pratirupa* and *Chakshusi* are her shadow images. There are two nymphs, *Amba* and *Ambayavi*. There are two rivers, *Ambaya*, in the image of knowledge. One who attains this knowledge, reaches *Brahmalok*. When *Brahmaji* orders that enlightened soul to be presented before him he reaches *Viraja* river that soul loses its old age for ever. On orders from *Brahmaji* 500 nymphs come to receive him, and welcome him with saffron, turmeric and vermilion. Now he crosses the pond of water, named *Aar*, but he will sink in it, if there is even a small shred of ignorance in him. When he comes near gods like *Yeshtiha*, they find it difficult to stand before him or face his glow, He leaves behind all his sins in *Viraja* river, and crosses it. In this way, the description of the path of *Devayan* is given in a beautiful manner. Just as a man riding a chariot can see its wheel moving, but cannot judge their impact on the ground, in the same way a man sees the coming and going of day and night, sins and piety but does not judge their impact. In other words, he sees his good and bad deeds as he sees the wheels of chariot, but does not come in their direct contact. Or to be more clear and specific, the man (soul) remains untouched by affections, illusions, anger and ego, he attains the knowledge of *Brahma* and becomes one with it.

Later on, when he reaches in front of *Ilya* tree he senses *Brahma-gandha* (divine scent) in himself, feels and tastes divine *Brahma rasa* on reaching *Sajalya* town, and enters into the glow of *Brahma* on reaching *Aparajit Ayatan* (the name of the godly abode of *Brahmaji*). The watchmen open the gate for him, and when he reaches *Vibhupramati* then the glory of Brahma enters him. He gets divine intelligence and significance on reaching *Vichakshana*. When he reaches *Amitauj*, the seat or bedstead of *Brahmaji*, he sees the past and future in its front bed posts and *Shree* and *Ishwari* in it back bed-posts. The boards placed there from east to west, and north to south are symbolic of the *Rig*, the *Sam* and the *Yajurveda*. The moon beams from the bed, and *Om* (*Udgeetha*) is the bedsheet on it.

Brahmaji sits relaxed on it. It is here that the soul sees

Brahmaji face to face.

When that soul (*Brahma vetta*) starts climbing the bed, then *Brahmaji* asked him, "who are you?"

Then the soul should reply in this manner:

Soul: "I am a season like spring. I originate from *Parabrahma*. I am also the same what you are."

Brahmaji: "Who am I?"

Soul: "The Truth."

Brahmaji: "What is the truth?"

Soul: "You are the truth incarnate. You are a truth more wonderful than life and divinity. Truth is divinity, and life is truth. The word 'truth' uttered by the voice is a combination of all these things. Truth is what all is. Everything is inherent in you. Therefore, you are the truth."

Brahmaji: "If you address me in a masculine gender, how will you call or pronounce?"

Soul: "Through *Pran* (life)."

Brahmaji: "If you address me in a feminine gender, then how?"

Soul: "Through voice (*Vani*)."

Brahmaji: "If you address me in a neuter gender, then how?"

Soul: "Through *Man* (mind)".

Brahmaji: "How do you experience scent?"

Soul: "Through the nose, the sense of smell."

Brahmaji: "How do you experience and infer forms?"

Soul: "Through eyes."

Brahmaji: "How do you hear the word?"

Soul: "Through ears."

Brahmaji: "How do you taste food grains?"

Soul: "Through tongue."

Brahmaji: "How do you act?"

Soul: "Through hands."

Brahmaji: "How do you experience happiness and pain?"

Soul: "Through body."

Brahmaji: "How do you enjoy the happiness of sexual consummation and child-birth?"

Soul: "Through penis i.e. through a sense."

Brahmaji: "How do you perform the activity of walking?"

Soul: "Through both legs."

Brahmaji: "How do you partake intelligence, tendencies,

knowable objects, and intentions?"

Soul: "Through *Pragya* (cognitive sense)."

Being satisfied with all the above answers, Brahmaji says: "Water etc., the five elements, are my places. This *Brahmalok* too has the predominance of water. Now you also reside here because you have attained *Brahma-gyan* (divine knowledge)."

In this way Maharshi Chitra imparted divine knowledge to Maharshi Udyalok. Udyalok Rishi felt obliged on receiving this knowledge, and then paying obeisance to the *Rishi*, he returned to his *Ashram* with this son.

This divine knowledge is not meant for Rishi Udyalok, but in this *Upnishad* it is meant for all men. How does a man acquire knowledge, saving himself from affections, illusions, anger, ego, deceit, fraud, lust and greed and moves across the ocean of the world? And how does he acquire the subtle knowledge of *Brahma* through his pure, unadulterated questions? You will find all this knowledge in this *Upnishad*.

Second Chapter: This chapter deals with the worship of *pran*, practical uses of the divine knowledge, freedom from sins, wishing (and praying) well for one's son, attainment of salvation, wealth etc.

Worship of Pran: In the beginning of this chapter *Kaushitaki Rishi* called *pran* as *Brahma* and described him as king. He has made his heart a messenger, voice the queen, eyes the minister, and ears the watchman. Gods have gifted us all the senses without our as king. *Maharshi* Pengaprastha, too, has called *pran* as Brahma. He said that senses such as eyes are beyond voice of *Brahma*. Eyes have surrounded voice (sound) on all four sides. Ears are beyond eyes. They have surrounded eyes on all sides. Heart surrounds eyes. Therefore, one gets happiness, prosperity, etc. through the worship of *pran*.

Worship for Wealth: One should organize and perform *yajna* (*anushtha*) for it. Aspirant for wealth, on a moonless or full moon night, or on some other auspicious date, should, after establishing fire and immersing *kusha* in *mantra* charmed water, offer the *ahuti* of ghee in this manner: "Goddess, who grants the desired boon should give me wealth. This *ahuti* is for you. '*Tasyai Svaha*'. *Pran* god, capable of granting the desired boon, should shower wealth on me—the aspirant." Likewise, praying to eye, ear, heart and *pragya* gods one should offer the following *ahuti*:

For eyes:

"*Chakshuvami devatavarodhini sa meamushmat idam avrundham tashai svaha.*"

Likewise one should offer *ahuti* to all gods.

After these *ahutis* one should smell the smoke, smear the remaining ghee on one's body and go about quietly for getting wealth. Then he will get the desired wealth.

Worship for controlling others: To get the desired result, to become dear to someone or to control someone, after establishing fire (as in the case of getting wealth) one should offer *ahutis* of ghee and pray in this way: "I take your voice in me in this way. *Tasyai svaha*". Likewise, one should offer *ahutis* for one's eyes, heart and subtle mind. For instance, for heart.

"*Manaste mayi juhaumyasau svaha*"

After this, scenting the smell of *dhoop*, smearing remaining ghee on one's body standing silent near the desired person, and entertaining the idea that he should be dear to him or be under his control, one should conduct oblation. And one will get the desired result.

Worship of the Sun: According to Kaushitaki *Rishi* one should worship the sun in the morning, noon, and in the evening. For this, touching one's *yagyopaveet*, taking an *achaman* (sip) of water one should offer water's *arghya* (offering) to the sun thrice, and one should recite *mantra* according to time. For instance, for morning—

"*Vargeasi papmanam me vridadhi*"

For noon time: "*Urdhargoasi papmanam me udvridadhi*"

For evening: "*Sambagoasi papmanam me samvridadhi.*"

i.e. in the morning, the sun god is called 'Aap varg' as he gives up the world like a straw. "O Sun, you are called *Aap varg*. You destroy my sins." For the noon, "O Sun God! You are *udvarg*. You destroy my sins." And for the evening, setting sun, "O Sun God! You are *savarg*. Remove my sins."

In this way, the sins of men committed during day and night are destroyed.

Worship of the moon: On does not suffer from the loss of son by this worship. In fact, one begets a son, if one is sonless.

On every moonless night, the moon is to the west of the Sun. One should keep green grass (*doob*) in a water-filled vessel and offer *arghya* to the moon in worship. Recite this mantra:

"*Yatte suseemam hridayamadhi chandramasiashritam*
Tena mritatvasyeshane maham pautramardyam rudam."

i.e. "O the Goddess with the halo of the moon! Your heart with beautiful thoughts resides in moon's halo. You are entitled to immortality. Kindly bless me. May I not weep in this world for loss of son."

With the recitation of this *mantra* one does not suffer from the loss of son. If one does not have a son, he should recite the following *mantra*, keeping green grass in a water filled vessel:

"*Apyayasva sametu te vishvatah somavrishnyam bhav vajasya*

Sam te payamsi samu yantu vaja se vrishnyanyabhi matishahah sangaye"

"*Apyayamanom amritaya som divi shrivansyuttamani dhishva.*

Yamaditya anshumapyapayanti yamakshitam kshitoyah pibanti."

Tin no raja varuno brihaspati shapyayayantu bhuwanasya gopa.

Masmank pranen pajaya pashubhirapyayayishtha yoasman dveshti."

"*Mam cha vayam dvippamastasya pranen prajaya pashubhirapyayayasva.*

Iti Devimavritamavarta aditasya vritamanwavarte iti."

This *mantra* is found in the 8th *sukta* of the second chapter. According to it, "You should grow by acquiring (attaining) the majestic glow of *Purush* (God). May the light, which is the cause of creation, establish itself. You are the bestower of food grains. O Moon of quiet qualities! Your *rasa* (beam) is good for flowers. It energises and conquers the enemies. It is easily available to those who live on food grains and water. Bestow fame on us through your light. May you establish glory in the *heaven*. May that moon, in the female form, who is cajoled and made happy by 12 *Adityas*, make us strong along with *Brihaspati*, endowed with unending strength. O Moon! Do not satiate your hunger by eating our subjects and animals, rather satisfy yourself from the life of our enemies, his children and his animals."

Worship of Som: On a full moon night, when you see the moon in front of you, you should pray in the below mentioned way. "O Som! You are a king. You have five, rare faces. You look after your subjects. Brahmins awaken *kshatriyas* and *kshatriyas* awaken *Vaishyas* with their one face only. These Brahmins and *Kshatriyas* are your one face each, through which you eat all birds and fires. May my *pran* (life), children and animals not be destroyed by your faces. On the other hand, kill and destroy the life, children and animals of our enemy."

One does not lose one's son, by worshipping Som this way.

Worship of *Pran* for attaining salvation: Here the worship of the life-element is described for attaining salvation. "Only *Brahma* (god) is brought out in whatever sounds a man makes. When he dies, then that light passes on to eyes, and *pran* merges into *pran*. When you see things through your eyes, this action of seeing is also *Brahma*. When the eyes die, this light (*pran*) reaches ears. When ears hear, they manifest *Brahma* in the act of hearing. When the ears die, they cannot hear. Then the light is received by mind. All the objects contemplated by mind, are also a form of *Brahma*. When the mind dies, contemplation stops. Then this light is received by *pran*. Therefore, all the gods experience satisfaction on entering into *pran*, and are not unconscious. And they begin again from here. One·who has this knowledge, his orders are complied with even by mountains. Those who are jealous are destroyed. This has been clarified by a story:

Once, due to ego, all the senses tried to prove themselves the best, and, therefore, they separated themselves from the body. As a consequence, the body died. But when all the senses re-entered their respective places in the body, then *pran* did not enter into it. Resultingly the body could not get up or do anything. However, when *pran* entered, the body sat up and stood. Then all the gods in the form of senses acknowledged *pran* as the highest and the best.

Therefore, a man, who attains this knowledge that *pran* itself is divine spirit and intelligence, and acknowledges its superiority, acquires heaven in the form of *Akash* after his death, and becomes immortal like the gods of heaven. The worship and knowledge of *pran* places a man face to face with *Brahma*, and the man attains salvation an acquiring this knowledge.

Successor to Father: This section describes how a father makes his son his successor.

When a father senses his end coming, then he wants to pass on his knowledge to his son. For this, the father should get a new shed of straw made, prepare fire, wear new clothes, and call his son to himself, and infuse him with all his energies of *pran*. He should touch different parts of his (son's) body and say, "I place in you my voice, *pran*, eyes, ears, best actions, happinesses, pains, pleasures of sex, desires, intelligence, strength, glory, light, health, virtures, *rasa* (essences), food grains, reproductive power, enlightened consciousness." The son, too, should accept and receive all these strengths of his father. A father attains heaven by doing this. If a father survives further, he should live under the shelter of his son. Or he should renounce, and take *sanyas*. In this way a son is made the successor to his father.

Third Chapter: In describes *pran*, senses and enlightened consciousness (*pragya*).

Pratardan, the son of king *Divodas*, reached heaven in order to help Indra, in a battle between the gods and demons. After the battle was over, Indra, being happy with his performance in the battle, told him to ask for a boon. Pratardan said, "kindly give me that which you consider is good for men."

On hearing this, Indra said, "O king! Ask a boon for yourself, not for all." Then the king said, "O Lord! I do not need any boon for myself."

Indra is truth personified. Therefore, he said, "O King! Recognise and understand my nature and form. Knowing me well is good for all, man and mankind, because a man who knows my true nature is untouched by sins—sins like killing people, patricide, theft etc.

Pragyua-Swarup Pran (Life as super intelligence): Exhorting Pratardan, Indra said, "I am *pran*. Worship me in the form of *pran*, *ayu*, and nectar, because *pran* alone is *ayu* and the element of immortality and as long as *pran* is there is body till then that man has his *ayu*. Therefore, when a man worships me as *pran* and immortality, he attains a full, long and complete life and the happiness in heaven. I am *pragya*, the super intelligence. This alone determines what is truth and falsehood. *Pran* is the most important thing in body, because man and other living beings live as long as *pran* is there in their bodies. The dumb also lives. The eyeless also lives. Likewise the deaf, mindless child, and the disabled or bereft live. But one who does not have *pran* cannot live. So, *pran* alone is worthy of worship.

"*Pran* alone is *pragya* (intellect), *Pragya* is *pran*. Both live in the body together, and go out of it together. So, when a man is about to die then he, bereft of energy and consciousness, does not recognize even known persons. At that time he neither says anything nor hears anything. Neither sees nor thinks. He is immersed in *pran* only; and names and forms all dissolve in *pran*. Again on taking re-birth all the five *pranas* (*pran, apan* etc) like sparks from fire, (partaking their true nature from soul in the form of *pran*) assume their respective places and their presiding gods and *loks* also manifest themselves.

"Thus *pran* is *pragya* and *pragya pran*. Both reside in the body together, and leave it together. Therefore, this is knowledge, this is *Brahma*."

Inter-relationship between *pran*, *pragya* and senses: *Pragya* is *pran* and *pran pragya*. All the senses are driven by *pragya*. Heart is related to *pran* and *pran* to *pragya*. Voice is a part of *pragya*. Another part is formed as nose which senses smell. Likewise, eyes, ears, tongue, hands, penis and legs—are different parts of *pragya* and have their separate, individual functions to perform. They respectively see forms, enjoy *rasa*, give, produce, help experience happiness and pain, sex, walking etc. Function of one part of *pragya* is performed by *pragya* itself, the external objects of which are the objects of experience such as desires and emotions, i.e. the experience of those objects is done by experiencing desires etc.

A living being, devoid of *pragya*, cannot cognize anything, because it is found that sometimes a man says that his mind/ attention was elsewhere. He could not follow what happened i.e. he was *pragyaless*.

Do not recognize voice, rather recognize soul which speaks out the voices. Do not know the smell, rather recognize the soul that accepts smell. In the same way, do not recognize other various activities, rather recognize the soul that directs or accepts them.

Pran alone is ageless, immortal, blissful and *pragyatma* (consciousness-soul). It does not grow big or small through big or mean deeds. *Parameshwar* (God), in the form of *pragya* and *pran*, assigns place to man in *loks* through noble deeds. It is the god of all, *lokpal* (governor), *lokadhipati* (owner of all places) i.e. *pran* imbued with these characteristics is the soul, and self knowledge leads to the knowledge of God.

Fourth Chapter: The energies and powers of the cosmos (*Brahmanda*) have been described in this chapter through a dialogue between a Brahmin named Gargya and Ajatshatru, the king of Kashi (Benaras). Gargya was the son of Rishi Balaka, and was well versed in the Vedas and other classics. His ashram was in a region named Ushinagar. He was used to touring and travelling. Once wandering through the states such as Mastsya, Kuru, Panchal, Videh etc. he reached Ajatshatru, the king of Kashi and said to him, "I will lecture and impart you knowledge about *Brahma.*"

On hearing this, Ajatshatru said, "I am really fortunate, I will give you a thousand cows for this."

Ajatshatru welcomed him warmly and profusely, got him lodged in a good *ashram.* Then a dialogue ensured between *Maharshi* Gargya and the king of *Kashi.*

Gargya said, "I worship the *Purush* (God) ensconced in *Aditya.*"

Ajatshatru said, "O Brahmin! This (God) draped in yellow clothes is certainly great. He is the best among all living beings. I also worship Him. One who worships him is the best among all living beings."

Gargya said, "I worship *Brahma* in *Purush* form ensconced in the glow of the moon."

Ajatshatru said, "O Brahmin! The moon is the king of all. It is the *pran* (life) of food grains. I worship him. One who worships Him in the form of *Brahma* himself becomes the spirit of food grains and becomes rich with wealth and food grains."

Gargya said, "I worship *Purush* in the form of *Brahma*, ensconced in the sphere of (electric) light."

Ajatshatru said, "O noble among Brahmins! I also worship this brilliance in the form of soul. One who worships in this manner becomes the spirit of brilliance, i.e. *Brahma* (soul) in the form of light."

Gargya said, "I worship *Parameshwar* in *Brahma* form, in hearing everything and ensconced on the cluster of clouds."

Ajatshatru said, "O noble Brahmin! I also worship Him,

taking Him as spirit. One who worships Him as the spirit of the word, himself becomes Spirit/Soul in word form."

Gargya: "I worship *Purush* in the spirit of *Brahma*, situated in the sky."

Ajatshatru: "O superior Brahmin! I worship Him, taking Him to be complete *Brahma*, minus Nature. One who worships Him in this way is gifted with progeny and cattle, and his children do not die pre-mature."

Gargya: "I am the worshipper of *Purush* situated in *vayumandal* (atmosphere)."

Ajatshatru, "O Brahmin! This alone is Indra. This is *Vaikuntha* (heaven, the abode of Vishnu). And this is unconquered, I worship Him in this spirit. His worshipper in this spirit remains invincible and scores victory over his adversaries."

Gargya: "I am a worshipper of Brahma in *Purush* form placed in fire."

Ajatshatru: "O Noble Brahmin! I also worship Him in that spirit."

Gargya: "I am a worshipper of *Purush*, placed in immense waters."

Ajatshatru: "O Noble Brahmin! It is the soul of all living beings. I worship him with this assumption. One who worships Him in this spirit becomes the soul of all living beings. It is divine worship (*adhidevik upasana*)."

Gargya: "I worship in the form of *Brahma* that *Purush* who is situated/placed in this mirror."

Ajatshatru: "O superior Brahmin! It is not like this. This is just a reflection/image. I worship Him in the form of image. One who worships Him in this spirit himself becomes His image. In other words, His worshipper acquires the qualities of reflection. His children, too, reflect this form."

In this way, it is stated that a man should have the knowledge of the soul. One should know the soul. It is the soul, the spirit which directs and controls man's all parts, organs and senses. So one who knows the soul knows *Brahma* also, and he attains immortality. He becomes significant and occupies higher positions. He becomes sinless, and attains salvation."

(5) Akshamalika Upnishad

The recital of peace in this Upnishad goes like this:

"*Om Vangme manasi prativishthata mano mem vachi pratishthatamavirma,*

Edhi, Vidasya na anistha shrutam me ma

Prahasirninathi tenahoratratsanddhamyamatam vadishyami

Satyam Vadishyami Tanmayaratu. Tadvaktarmatu.

Avatu bham, Avatu Vaktaramavatu

Om Shantih, Shantih, Shantih"

i.e. "Let my voice be in heart, and my heart in my voice—O (God in the) Form of Light! Appear before me. O voice and heart! You are the basis of our knowledge of the *Vedas*. Therefore, do not strike at our knowledge of the *Vedas*. I am immersed day and night in their studies. I speak the truth, and my words reflect the reality around. Protect me. Protect the speaker. Protect both of us. May all the (three) sins subside."

Just there are strings of the beads of ruby, *rudraksha* and *Tulsi*; likewise there is an *aksharmala* (string), made of 'a' to 'ksha'. It is called *aksharmala*. For this reason, it is called *Aksharmalika Upnishad*. It describes different kinds of strings; the discussion between *Prajapati* and *Guh* has been arranged in a string form. Its different forms, varieties, characteristics and threads have been narrated. In this dialogue, *Prajapati* asks questions and wants to know the methods and various kinds of *aksharmala*. What are its characteristics? What varieties? How many threads? How are they knitted and woven? How many shades? What is their significance? Who are their presiding gods? What results do they offer?

Then *Guh* (Kartikeya) replies: "There are ten kinds of strings, of ruby (*praval*), pearl, marble, conch, *Tulsi*, gold, sandalwood, *putrajeeva*, lotus and *rudraksha*. They are taken, accepted with the spirit of letters from 'a' to 'ksha'. Threads of gold, silver and copper are used for them. Gold around it, silver on the left side, face in face (interlaced) and *putra* are inner threads. Brahma is their last thread. Its right part, left part, face, tail, head and knots are respectively *Shaiva, Vaishnav, Saraswati, Gayatri, Vidya* (knowledge) and Nature (*Prakriti*). The white beads are sound, and the yellow reflect touch.

Before wearing they should be washed in scented water, purified with *panchagavya* and the milk of five cows (*Nanda* etc.—cow of rare characteristics). They should be washed using a *kurcha* (small ladle) of leaves, along with the chanting of 'Om'. Then they should be smeared with eight scents. Then placing them on a white stone, flowers should be offered to them reverentially. Then each bead should be charmed with *mantras* in this way, using letters from 'a' to '*ksha*' – 'O Om a! You are omnipresent and have overcome death. Enter into this first bead (pearl) '*Aa*'! You are attractive in nature and your access is everywhere. You enter the second bead. *Om E!* You are free from regrets, and you are a nurturer. Enter this third bead. In this way, beginning with 16 vowels such as *ri, lri, an, ah* etc. and 34 consonants all are invoked. *Mantras* are invoked for every bead. All this *anushthan* involves detailed *karma-kand.* (All cannot be described, because in ritual worship only the basic *mantra* is recited. Therefore, this *karma-kand* should be executed through the basic *mantras*.)

Later on pray to God, contemplating in this way: "My salutations to gods wandering over the earth! All of you place yourself in this string. Ratify and strengthen it. May the departed souls, too, should grace it. Give their assent. Forefathers, such as *Anishvat* too, should support this bead of strings, charmed with knowledge. My salutations to gods residing in the sky! They should support and grace this knowledge-based string of beads. My obeisance to all the *mantras* and existent knowledge. The strengths and energies of all of them should enter and find a place for themselves in this string. My salutations to manifest Brahma, Vishnu and *Rudra*! My salutations to philosophies such as that of *Samkhya* school of thought. All of you should come and find a place for yourself in this string. My salutations to hundreds and thousands of followers of Vishnu and *Shakti.* They should also support. My salutations to the life-protecting powers of death. May they bless me!"

Taking this string to be endowed with all virtues, the beads should be stringed. Using the method, all the 50 beads are again stringed. The remaining 8 beads, '*a*', '*ka*', '*cha*', '*ta*', '*tha*', '*pa*', '*ya*', and '*sha*' should also be charmed with *mantras* as narrated above. In this way a string of 108 beads should be prepared.

When the string is ready, one should go round it and pray to it. "*Bhagawati Akshamala* (O Goddess string)! You control all. My salutations to you! O string, mother of *mantras*! You surprise all. My salutations to you! Mother of *mantras*, *Akshamala*! You distract others! You are the death to all. You are the conqueror of Death also (Lord Shiva!) You agitate, excite all. You are a rare world. You always light the path. You protect all the worlds. Giver of Life! Producer of all! You cause day and night. You reside in hearts. You go from one river to another, from one country to another, and from one continent to another. You have an other worldly form. My salutations to you! O visible form! My salutations! O middle form! My salutation! (*Para*, *Pashyanti*, *Madhyama*, and *Vaikhari*—these are various forms of sound). O *Vaikhari* form! Salutations! The spirit of all! All knowledge! All powers! Mother in the form of gods! Salutations! You have been worshipped by Muni Vashishtha. You have been served by Muni Vishwamitra. Therefore, I salute you."

One who studies this *Upnishad* in the morning is freed from the sires of night. By studying it in the evening, one is freed from the sins of the day. Even a sinner is redeemed if he studies it in the morning and evening. Lord *Guh* (Kartikeya) said that the recital of a *mantra* on this string bestows upon a man the desired fruits very soon.

(6) *Bahavricha Upnishad*

This *Upnishad* of the *Rig-Veda* describes the worship of *Devi Kam Kala*, as the maker of this creation, i.e. the Goddess of Prime Forces (*Adyashakti Devi*) who is called *Chitta-shakti* (heart and mind combined) also. *Brahma*, Vishu and Rudra also originated from her. The description goes like this –

Before the creation, there was only *Devi*, the Goddess. She created the world. She is known by the name of *Kam Kala* and *Shringar Kala*. It was she who created Vishnu, Brahma, Rudra, Gandharva, *Marudganas*, nymphs and *kinnaras*. She created all objects, moving and non-moving, useful things, all kinds of living beings and human beings. She is *apara shakti*, i.e. the power in the world. She is all kinds of studies and knowledge, such as *Shambhavi*. She is the basic elements, non-aging and non-destructible. She is inherent in all three kinds of bodies (solid, subtle and causal) and all the three states (dream, wakefulness and sleep). Though present in all places and times, (time and distances), she remains untouched by them. She pervades all in the form of consciousness. She alone is the soul. The rest is all untrue. She helps you realize *Brahma*, i.e.

she is the truth, consciousness and bliss. That *Tripur Sundari* (the most beautiful in all the three *loks*) is pervasive both inside and outside. She herself is in the form of light. You, I and the gods in the world everything is *Tripur Sundari* herself. *Bhagawati Lalita* (the Goddess Beautiful) alone is the truth. She alone is *Para-Brahma.* The supreme element is that which remains there (by way of deduction) after giving up being and non-being, and assumes form.

The superior or high knowledge itself is *Brahma.* The same *Brahma* is described in sentences 'I am *Brahma.*' 'The soul permeating the body is *Brahma,*' i.e. '*Ayamatma Brahma*' or '*Tatvamasi*' i.e. 'thou art that'. One should try to know him. These words describe '*Brahma vidya*' the supreme knowledge. This god is satisfied with the invocation and recital of the 15-letter *mantra* of '*Shodashi Shree Vidya*'. Her other names are as follows: *Shri Maha-Tripur Sundari, Tiraskarini, Ambika, Rajmatangi, Shukrshyamala, Chandi, Laghushyamala, Ashwarudha, Pratyangira, Dhumavati, Savitri, Saraswati, Bala, Gayatri, Brahmanand, Kala.*

Sky is a place which has no beginning, no end. All gods and *richas* live there. His life is futile who is not aware of them or who does not try to know them. One who knows them reaches there and live with them. In other words, that man, after knowing them and becoming *Brahma-gyani,* lives there with Gods.

(7) Saubhagya Lakshmi Upnishad

The peace invocation of this *Upnishad* is:

"*Om vangme manasi pratishtha, mano me vachi pratishthamavira virmaedhi*
Vedasya ma anisthah shrutam me ma prahasih
Anenedhikenahoratran tsandadhamyritam vadishyami!
Satyam Vadishyami Tanmamaatu. Tadvaktaramavatu, Avatu mamavatu. Vaktaramavatu Vaktaram.
Om shantih, shantih, shantih!"

i.e. "O God! May my voice be placed in my heart! My heart in my voice. You appear before me. Give me the knowledge of the *Vedas.* Let me not forget what I have heard. Let me devote my days and nights in this study. Let me speak the truth. Protect me, Protect my *guru.* Protect both of us. All kinds of pains (of body, physical and god given) should subside."

This *Upnishad* of the *Rig Veda* describes the *Vedic karma kand* to acquire Lakshmi (wealth, and its goddess). This *Upnishad* is divided into three parts: The *Shri sukta* (the *mantra* of Goddess Lakshmi), comprising of 15 *richas*, is described here. It is believed that if someone, performing *yajna*, making offerings of ghee in this *yajna* for fifteen days, invokes these *richas* then he gets wealth.

First Part

The *Saubhagya Lakshmi* knowledge, *Lakshmi mantra* and *chakra* find mention here.

Once upon a time all the gods discussed the issues related to wealth with Shri Narayan. He told them: "Listen carefully, everybody. She (Laxmi) sits not on the seat in *Turiya* (trance) state but in a state created by *mantras* beyond *turiya* (solid subtle and *causal*) state. This seat and sub-seats are surrounded and graced by gods. Such four-handed Lakshmi should be contemplated by reciting *Shri Sukta* comprising of 15 *richas*. The formulators of these *richas* are Rishi Angira, Anand, Kardam and Chivaleet."

According to the 4th *shloka* of this part, "seated on a red lotus flower, Lakshmi, more beautiful than the pollen of lotus, appears in a fearless state. She has fresh lotuses in her hands and she is adorned by precious stones such as ruby. Such Mother Saraswati, the owner of all abodes, should enrich us with *Shri* (wealth)."

In other words, Lakshmi should add to our good luck, wealth and abundance. The secret of worship of Lakshmi is enshrined in this *mantra*, Lakshmi, as a power, is worshipped by various names such as *Varada* (bestower of boons), *Vishnupriya* (the beloved of Lord Vishnu). But only those succeed in this knowledge of *shree* (wealth) who worship her in a detached manner. One does not succeed if one proceeds with pre-determined aims and desires.

Second Part

Pranayam yoga, gyan yoga are described in this part. When the gods enquired about the elements of *turyia maya*, Shri Narayan said, "*Yoga* only leads to growth of *yoga*. So know *yoga* through *yoga* itself. A careful practitioner of *yoga* enjoys happiness for a longer period. Controlling one's sleep, eating less, the yogi sits alone in a convenient place and practises *pranayam.* Strongly drawing air through mouth, he joins it to his navel with *apan vayu* (non-inhalable air). Then closing his ears, eyes and nose with his thumb, fingers and palms, the *yogi* in his *pranayam* contemplates *pranav* (God) and comes (realizes) face to face with his soul. Practising it slowly and slowly one reaches a state wherein on hears the unheard sound of *pranav* from *sushumna* (a centre of nerves). Inspired by the unheard sound, *pran,* piercing through *muladhar charka* (the fundamental centre) enters into *sushumna.* One sits with ease in *padmasan,* pierces through *Vishnu granthi* and enjoys bliss. When *pran* rubs against nerves, then the sound of bugle is heard, and on piercing *mani chakra* the sound of *mridanga* (a percussion instrument) is heard. When the *pran vayu* reaches the ultimate void, then one realizes all successes and when it (*vayu*) pieces *talu chakra,* then the heart experiences happiness and concentration.

At the end of *sadhana* (devotional practice) *pranav* (God) Himself is created in word form. Then the *chith* is lost in Him. This physical body of *maya* is dedicated to *Brahma.* Only that person is a *yogi* who perceives soul as pervading all. He alone can perform *yoga.* He reaches a (detached) state of *Samadhi* or salvation. He is freed of ego and *maya, Samadhi* is the dissolution of soul in God, like salt in water. In other words, the union of soul with *chith* is *Samadhi.* The vacuity felt in heart and mind and the realization of a painless state is *Samadhi.* The fixity of heart and the contemplative state of mind, even though the body is in action, is also *Samadhi.*

In this state, wherever the heart wanders, it finds *Brahma* only. He realizes *Brahma* in the state of *Samadhi.* The state can be reached through *pranayam.* The aspirant or *yogi* experiences great happiness. He is freed from pains.

Third Part

Navchakras (nine cycles) are described in this part. When gods asked about these nine cycles, Shri Vishnu said, "*Brahma-chakra* located in the *muladhar* (basic centre) has three rings about it. One should contemplate of *Kundalini shakti* (cyclical power) there in *mul kand* (basic nectar), which is like fire. There *is kamrup peetha* there. It fulfils all desires. The second is *swadhishthan chakra.* One should contemplate of red *linga* facing west, and located in a lotus of 6 leaves. This is the *uddayan peetha* which grants you *siddhi* (success) of attracting the world. The third is *nabhi-chakra*, and it is zigzag like a snake. One should contemplate of *Kundalini* (in it) like lightning and crores of śuns rising. Once *Kundalini* is awakened, it is highly powerful and brings all kinds of success. The fourth is *Manipurak* or heart *chakra*. One should contemplate of *hans kala* (white movements like those of a swan) like *jyotirmaya linga* here. It controls all the *loks*. *Kantha chakra* is barely four fingers thick. For it, one should contemplate of *ira* in left, *pingla* in right side with *sushumna* in the centre.

Talu-chakra is like the flow of nectar like thumb. By contemplating of (a lamp's) flame of knowledge you realize the success of voice. *Brahmarandhra* is the *nirvana-chakra*. Here contemplate on a line of smoke like the eye of a needle. This is *jalandhar peetha*, granting salvation.

The ninth is the sky (*Akash*) *chakra*. There one should contemplate of *shakti* (power) inclined towards a three-leafed *karnika* (flower) in the midst of a 16-leafed lotus. This is complete *giri-peetha*. An aspirant achieves *siddhi* (success) on piercing through these nine *chakras* and reaches God.

An aspirant, by studying this *Upnishad* daily, becomes pure like fire and air, and achieves salvation, along with wealth, property, woman, son, animals and servants.

(8) *Radha Upnishad*

Shanti path of this *Upnishad* is—
"*Om purnamadah purnamidam purnatpurnamudachyate*
Purnasya purnamaday purnamevav shishyate
Om Shantih, Shantih, Shantih"
i.e., "*Brahma* is complete. This world is also complete. This complete world has originated from that complete *Brahma*. So, if you separate this complete world from that complete *Brahma*, then what remains is also complete."

In this *Upnishad* of the *Rig-veda*, Brahmaji has called Shri Krishna as the first god, and his *shakti* (strength), Shri Radha is called the best *shakti*. 28 names of Radhaji are mentioned here. After worship, *Rishis* like *Sanak* asked of Brahmaji, "O Lord! Who is the highest god? What are his strengths? And which of those strengths are a cause of this creation?"

Brahmaji said, 'Sons, this is the ultimate mystery. One

should not talk about it to anyone and all. If you tell this to an incompetent person, other than a deserving *Brahmachari*, who is devoted to his *guru*, you invite sin. Listen, Lord Shri Krishna is the Supreme God. He is endowel with six peculiar luxuries. He is served by his cowherd boys and girls and worshipped by the people of Vrindaban. This Lord of Vrindaban is the only God. This Narayan is the master of all worlds. He is the perennial *Purush* described in the *Puranas*. He has many strengths such as those to grant happiness, search, knowledge, action etc. *Ahladini* (happiness-causing) *shakti* is the best of all. That *shakti* is Radha. The (strength) *shakti* that permeates his innermost being is famous as Shri Radha. Shri Krishna also worships her. This Radha is called Gandharva as well. Lakshmiji is also born of her. Though she is integral part of Shri Krishna, she has divided herself into two forms, Radha and Krishna, for the sale of various loving activities of Shri Krishna.

She is the all-powerful Goddess of all-powerful Shri Krishna. She is perennial knowledge, and is the goddess of the *pran* (life) of Shri Krishna. Deities contemplate her with great concentration. No one can follow her movements. You can assume that that person attains salvation with whom she is happy. A person worshipping Shri Krishna, without knowing her, is a fool of the first order. The *Vedas* also sing of her 29 names, which are—

Shri Radha, Raseshwari, Ramya, Krishnamantradihidevata, Sarvadha, Sarvavandya, Vrindabanviharini, Rama, Vrindaradhya, Asheshgopimandalpujita, Satya, Styapara, Satyabhama, Shrikrishnavallabha, Vrishabhanusuta, Gopi, Mul Prakriti, Iswari, Purna Gandharva, Radhika, Aramya, Rukmini, Paratpara, Parameshwari, Purnachandranibhanana, Bhukti muktiprada, and Bhavayadhivighna-vinashini.

One who recites these names is freed from the cycle of life. The *sandhini shakti* comprises of home, ornaments, bed, friend, servant etc. Will power is *Maya*. This *shakti* comprising of 3 *gunas* (*satva, raja* and *tama*) is the cause of this world. By transforming itself into ignorance, it plunges a man into bondages. The action power is the *leela shakti* of the Lord.

A person, studying this *Upnishad*, gets into a regular life, and becomes pure like the wind and other gods. Wherever he sees, his sight purifies all as he is dear to Radha and Krishna.

(9) *Nirvana Upnishad*

This *Upnishad*, related to the *Rig Veda*, describes how the highly advanced soul has attained ultimate freedom (salvation). Besides, who is a *sanyasin*? It describes how he received the message of life, alms, and a glimpse of gods.

It analyses what is the knowledge of salvation. That is why it is stated that *sanyasin* is one who collects resources for attaining salvation. His soul is his *Rishi*. Salvation is his God. Like the sky, his aim is that he does not desire anything.

Like the various, inter-playing waves and currents of a river the soul itself is *sanyasin*. Its nature is one of salvation. Her nature is free from *Maya*. To exercise for a higher state of being is the place of his worship. Meeting and merging in *Brahma* is his life-message. Freedom from the world is his exhortation. Pure satisfaction is his string of happiness. Patience is his sheet cover. Indifference to the world is his *kaupin* (bare clothes). Thought is his guiding staff. The yoga which leads him to God is his guarantee. Wooden *chappals* are his property, The desire for God is his conduct, and *Kundalni* is his bond. He becomes free in life just by not speaking ill of others.

Brahma is devoid of all the three *gunas*. Heart and voice can attain him only through discretion and wisdom. A person born in this transitory world lives as if in a dream, or is like an elephant which has been crafted for deceiving others. This body is like a snare of *maya*, or an illusion in which a man considers rope a snake. Brahma, known by hundreds of names such as Vishnu, Brahma etc, is the ultimate object and to control one's heart is the way to realize Him.

A *Sanyasin* should eat only the food he has begged. A lonely place is his monastery. He should fellow the exhortations of *Brahma* and spread this knowledge. Like the *Vedas*, he should control his senses. He should not disrespect anybody, because this is his pure strength. His daily lifestyle should be such as to destroy affection, *maya* and ego. He spends his time in searching a state of being devoid of all three *gunas*. His clothes are old and tattered. His conduct is like a boat carrying him to *Para-Brahma*.

One studies quietly during *Brahmacharya ashram*; and again in *Vanpratha ashram* one studies. But the *Sanyas ashram* is different from all others. Coming face to face with salvation is inherent in destroying one's all doubts by becoming complete *Brahma*. This knowledge should be imparted to one's son and disciple only and to none else.

(10) *Atmabodh Upnishad*

It has 2 chapters. One is exhorted to worship 'Aum'. Additionally it describes how to reach *Vaikunthadham, chakra, conch, padma*, club of Shri Hari.

First Chapter: It is stated that one can reach *Vaikuntha* by reciting, "Om namo Narayan." The three letters 'a', 'u' and 'm' directly present *Pranav*, the *Anand-Brahma Purush*. This *Pranav* is called 'Aum'. One who recites it becomes a *yogi* and free from the cycles of birth and death, and the bondages of the world. If you want to reach the *Vaikunthadham* of Lord Narayan who holds *chakra*, conch and club in his hand, then you should worship Him reciting the following *shloka*:

"*Om namo Narayanaya shankha charka gadadharaya tasmat*

Om namo Narayanayeti mantropasako Vaikuntha bhuvanam gamishyati."

"O Lord! Holding conch, *chakra* and club! My salutations to your *Narayan* form. By reciting your *mantra*—'Om Namo Narayana' one reaches *Vaikuntha lok*."

The heart in this body, in a lotus form, is *Brahmapuri*, the abode of the Lord. In this resides Shri Vishnu, the son of Devki, Madhusudan, Pundarikaksha, the unfalling and the unfailing. Like a lamp, he is always lit up. He is the well-wisher of Brahmins and those who have the knowledge of *Brahma*. A benefactor. He is *Purush, Virat* (immense) and Causelesss. He is *Para Brahma 'Aum'*.

One who remembers Shri Vishnu in this form is freed from affections and sorrows. He is a duality, non-duality and both. One who does not know him is ignorant, and is born again and again in this world and passes through 84 lakh forms of being. But one who has this knowledge reaches *Vaikuntha lok* and is free from the cycles of birth and death.

Brahma residing in our heart is the essence knowledge, the eye of the learned, Knowing Him, satiates a man's all desires, and he attains immortality on reaching heaven, after leaving this world.

The sum and substance is: with the worship of Shri Vishnu

a man attains freedom from affection, *maya* and the cycles of birth and death. Then his only desire is to be near the everlasting light and at a place where worship goes on all around, all the time. He wants a place for himself in that immortal *lok*.

Second Chapter: This chapter deals with ego and describes how ego, i.e. 'I' can be destroyed. A man knowing God through self-knowledge, an aspirant realizing his soul, is freed from ego, and he attains the following knowledge.

"For me the bondages of affection and *maya* exist no more. My 'I' is finished, over. The difference between soul and God is there no more. All the rules and prohibitions have ended for me. I have abjured religion. I am the most happy person as I have the ultimate knowledge. I am stable, ageless, immortal unending, above all kinds of partisanships. I am knowledge itself. I am an ocean of bliss and salvation. I am subtle, undecaying. All the three *gunas*—*satva, raja* and *tama*—have come to an end for me. I am the highest consciousness, perennial, pure, eternal. I am well placed in the highest bliss, glory and status of God.

"My discretionary wisdom tells me that the soul enjoys non-duality, and all bondages, emancipation and conduct appear one and the same. Once out of illusion, a man does not take rope for a snake; likewise when illusions of *maya* drop down, one sees only *Brahma* all around. Like the sweetness in the sugarcane, I am, also spread over all the three *loks*. From *Brahma* to the smallest insect and worms—I inhere everything. I do not have craving for anything in the world. While choosing between poison and nectar, one gives up poison; likewise after realizing my soul, I have given up non-soul.

"The soul is not destroyed with the end of the body in the same way as with the breaking of (water-filled) pitcher— (reflecting the sun in its water), the sun, which lights it, is not destroyed. It is body which is subjected to death, and not the soul which is immortal. It remains. Body is like the pitcher which breaks and is destroyed, but the sun, (the soul, informing it), the lighting agent is not destroyed. Now bondages, emancipation, guru or *shastras*—they are nothing to me now. Let the *pran* (life) go. Let happiness go experiencing heart, with all the appendages of karmas go. Now nothing makes me sad. In other words, I will not be unhappy, or sad with the departure of all joys, *pran* etc. because they are all ephemeral.

In other words, I will not be sad on losing everything, because I have attained the highest bliss through self-knowledge.

"My ignorance has come to an end. I have known the nature of soul. Family status, the title of being a Brahmin, name, beauty etc.—all there things are for the physical body. But the soul is beyond all these things, and I have known it. Likewise hunger, thirst, lust, anger etc. too, are related to body, but now I am free from them all. Just as an owl sees darkness (only) in light, likewise an ignorant person does not (cannot) see *Paramatma*. Just as nectar is not affected by poison, likewise I am beyond (uninfluenced) by these physical, worldly things. In other words, I am not subjected to worldly affections, and *maya* any more. A rope is a rope, and not a snake. Likewise I have known the true form of body, attained the true knowledge about soul."

A man is redeemed of the cycles of birth and death, if he remembers the message of this *Upnishad* even for a fraction of a second.

The Upnishads Related to Shukla Yajurveda

There are two parts of the *Yajur-veda*: *Shukla Yajur-veda* and *Krishna Yajurveda*.

Main *Upnishads* related *Shukla Yajurveda* are:

(1) *Ishavasya Upnishad*, (2) *Adhyatma Upnishad* (3) *Shiva-sankalpa Upnishad* (4) *Niralamba Upnishad* (5) *Turiyateet Upnishad* (6) *Subal Upnishad* (7) *Mandal Brahman Upnishad* (8) *Hans Upnishad* (9) *Paingal Upnishad* (10) *Shatyayaniya Upnishad* (11) *Yagyavalkya Upnishad* (12) *Jabal Upnishad* (13) *Paramhans Upnishad* (14) *Bhikshuk Upnishad* (15) *Trishikh Brahman Upnishad* (16) *Advayatarak Upnishad* (17) *Brihadaranyak Upnishad*.

(1) *Ishavasya Upnishad*

The peace-chant (*Shanti-path*) of this *Upnishad* is—

"*Om purnamadah purnamidam purnatpurna mudachyate |
Purnasya purnamadaya purnamevavashishyate | |* "

i.e. 'that Brahma is complete in himself. This action world is also complete. This completeness is born of that completeness. Therefore, when this complete (total) is taken out from that complete, then what is left is also complete.'

This *Upnishad* is assigned the first place among *Upnishads* because it is not separate from *Samhita*. Rather it is the 40th chapter of *Shukla Yajurveda*. In other words, it is included in the *Vedas*. It deals with the attributes, form of *Paramatma*, and the true knowledge about *Para Brahma* and *Paramatma*.

What is *Para Brahma*?

All living beings have a common soul. Dogs, cats etc. also have the same soul as man. i.e. *Para Brahma* is the knowledge of the soul in the form of any (one) living being. In other words, the self knowledge of one's own self is *Para Brahma*.

What is *Parameshwar*?

When the description of some form is made in relation to the whole cosmos; i.e. the entire universe of moving and non-moving beings, then He (that FORM) is *Parameshwar*.

This *Upnishad* has ony 18 *shlokas*.

"*Om ishavasyamidam sarvam yatkincha jagatamjagat|
Tentyenken bhunjeetha ma gridhah kasya sviddhanam||*"

According to this *shloka*, "In this changing world, God is inherent in all the fixed and moving things. Therefore, abjuring them, they should be used with a sense of renunciation/ detachment. One should not crave for what one does not have. Reason, whose wealth is this? Of none."

The sense of other *shlokas* is as follows:

Once born in this world, one should perform most intensely and courageously and desire to live for a hundred years. Thus one should conduct oneself according to this and the earlier *shloka*. Besides this, there is no other path of one's upliftment. Those persons remain untainted from the ill effects of actions who, in the course of enjoyment of all worldly pleasures, do not forget their duties and desirable actions.

Those persons are totally lost in ignorance who indulge in the show of their brute physical strength, who indulge in violence and hurting others; who are incapable of understanding the ideal human way of living; and those who follow the path of falsehood and untruth. They only hurt and kill themselves. These self-killers, after death, are born in the spheres of demons. *Brahma* is not mercurial. He is ageless, invigorating faster than man's heart and mind, and beyond the senses like eyes, tongue, ears etc. The foetus in mother's womb, on the basis of the same *Brahma*, will reap the fruits of his earlier actions.

Brahma makes move all things in the world, provide them speed, but in Himself. He is not moving, fickle. He is with the wise, beyond the reach of the ignorant persons. He is both inside and outside the whole fixed and moving world. The wise see Him within themselves, whereas the ignorant do not see him anywhere.

The wise, knowledgeable person who perceives the soul in the form of a part, a spark of *Paramatma* in all living beings, men and animals, is liked by all, He does not hate anyone.

Once a man reaches that state of mind when he perceives soul in all objects, he is freed from all affections.

Soul pervades all, is everywhere. It does not have a body. It is colourless, nerveless. It is free from sins, is full of glow. It is beyond the knowledge acquired through senses. It is in the nature of super meditation. It is victorious. It is self born. It has arranged, managed all the senses and their objects from time immemorial.

Those who treat soul as nothing live in the darkness of ignorance. But on the other hand those who are lost in their self-knowledge only are lost in ignorance darker than the ignorance of the worshippers of *avidya*. (In the *Upnishads*, *avidya* means the practice of *vaidyak* i.e. quack or fake medical profession, chemical and physical sciences, and *vidya* means spiritual knowledge).

Soul progresses through *vidya*, i.e. self-knowledge. One develops worldliness by *avidya*. Therefore, the results of both are different. Through *vidya* you gain spiritual strength whereas through *avidya* you make worldly progress. One who is equally conversant with both conquers over untimely death through *avidya*, and gains self-knowledge and immortality through *vidya*.

Those who talk of *asambhuti* (*separatism*) are in deep darkness, whereas the proponents of unitarianism (oneness) are in a deeper darkness. Therefore, the extremes of both *asambhuti* and *sanghavad* are not desirable. (The extreme of unitarianism destroys the freedom of an individual. These extremist thinking led to the rise of a dictator like Hitler who became the cause of a World War).

It is said that the results/consequences of following *sanghavad* and *asam bhuttivad* are different. One who knows the proper use of both saves himself from diseases and untimely death, and attains immortality by following *sanghavad*.

Comfortable availability and use of things deprive a man the knowledge of the truth. Indulgence in worldly things blocks one's awareness of the truth. "O God! You open for me the door (to truth) for observing the truth religiously. It is compulsory that one gives up one's craving for money and wealth in order to pursue true religion. Man's greed for wealth takes him astray from the path of truth. Therefore, O God! Save us from this greed."

"O nurturing seer, controlling brilliance! O God who looks after the welfare of his subjects! Draw to one side, into yourself, your brilliance. I find it difficult to see amidst this brightest glow, and I want to see that brilliance of yours which is entirely for the good of living beings. I am that devotee of yours who has assumed *pran* (life) in this body."

"Soul is unearthly, strengthening and in the nature of doling out immortality. In the end this body will be reduced to ashes (i.e. after death all its five elements will join respective elements and disappear). Therefore, O active man! Think of the actions you are performing. Think of the soul that protects all. O active man! Contemplate your actions."

"O God in the form of Fire! Take us to our self-realisation through the best path. O God! You know all our actions. You know everything. Please take away our mean sins, and free us from our misdeeds. Our salutations to you! We worship you."

The essence of all of this is: that a man realizes God, and gives up his affections and greed and sorrows. He distances himself from these things, and sees the play of God in all fixed and moving things. In other words, he sees God in everything. And having experienced and adopted this attitude, he becomes wise."

(2) *Adhyatma Upnishad*

This *Upnishad* provides a description of the soul element, and dilates upon the existence of God, *Para-Brahma* (though un-born) in all things. i.e. where is *Brahma*? In what form? Unborn *Brahma* (the eternal) resides in a cave known as body. The earth is his body, but the earth does not know it. Likewise, water, brilliance, sky, wind, heart, intellect, ego, consciousness, the unexpressed, letter and death etc. all are his body. The last residue in all is *Brahma*. But all are ignorant about it. He is the inner soul of all living beings. He is a divine body— *Narayana*, free from all sins. Body, eyes, senses are spiritual objects. I and mine—all this is illusion, because no one owns anything. The ignorant persons do not understand this. But the scholarly, wise persons, having faith in God, know and discover it.

This body is born of the faeces of mother and father and comprises of flesh and excreta. Give it up as the basest. Become Brahma and make yourself the real you are. Come face to face with *Brahma* inherent in your body. Be self-lighted, self-born and become *Brahma* and then give us this body, eggs (*andkosh*) and *Brahmanda* (cosmos) as a commode i.e. a pot containing faeces. Free yourself from the affection, greed and other worldly bondages. Direct the physical ego to supreme consciousness, which is ever blissful; give up body and feel only the feeling, essence. Once a man is rid of ego, he realizes his true self and becomes pure like *Brahma.* He is always happy and a light unto himself. Salvation lies in destroying actions, worries and passions. See *Brahma* in all things. Never be slack in learning—knowing the Supreme God. Slackness is the other name of death. Scale is formed in water. You remove it, and it is re-formed. In the same way, if you lose sight of *Brahma* your mind is covered again by *maya.* Once a man loses sight of God, he is again besmeared in the web of affections and greed.

Once a man is settled in the faith in *Brahma,* he remains there after death as well. Therefore, being settled in one's soul, one should realize it because Brahma, Vishnu, Mahesh, Indra etc. are also the soul itself. One should attain the experience of Brahma through the experience of soul.

All the existent things in the fixed and moving world are just a feeling, a glimpse only. Keeping a distance from them, or freedom from them makes a man a non-dualsim based *Para-Brahma.*

The root of salvation lies in one's *chitta,* or mind. There exists no salvation in the absence of mind. So one should directly apply one's mind to God. Once a man gives up the illusions of *maya* and *jeeva,* one sees *Para-Brahma* only. In this way, He is you yourself. When one hears such noble statements, it means one is hearing of the unity, oneness of *Brahma* and *jeeva,* i.e. God and the living being. When one thinks of what he has heard, it is called contemplation. *Samadhi* means being non-moving, like a lamp placed at an airless site. During *Samadhi* instincts and inclinations are unknown and are visible to soul only and when one comes out of *Samadhi,* he is slightly aware of them. Man performs many actions in the world, but when they are immersed in *Samadhi,* it improves and increases sense of *dharma.*

The aim of knowing should be a lack of passion for objects and the destruction of ego. A heart/mind lost in *Brahma* is inactive and free from all defeats/desires. Refined soul and *Brahma* are called unitarian, desireless intelligence and an aspirant, endowed with it is called *jeevan-mukta*—free, emancipated. Lack of affection for body, senses and other objects is also called *jeevan-mukta.* That person is also called *jeevan mukta* whose knowledge sees *jeeva* in *Brahma* and

Brahma in *jeeva* and who considers respect by good persons and torture by evil persons as one and the same. The world changes for the man who has realized *Brahma*. It is not the same it was before his realization. Just a person waking from a dream realizes the truth; likewise the realization 'Aham *Brahmasmi*' i.e. 'I am *Brahma*' destroys all the innumerable actions and their results which have kept a man enthralled for countless years, i.e. he knows reality and sheds illusions and worldly affections.

Soul is not affected by titles or other attributes. Once an arrow is shot, it does not stop short of its target. Likewise, after realization of God-soul, a man is freed from all old actional results (*prarabtha karmas*). They lose meaning for him.

Once a man has the knowledge of soul, as above the body, the actions of earlier lives become fruitful and successful. One should not be centred in body; in fact by abjuring it, one should give up one's accumulated part (*prarabdha*). It is just a hypothesis that the body is ours. It is not.

How is a lie born? Where from did we come to know of the un-born? Therefore, one that is not born is non-existent. How can that be one's *prarabdha*? Body is a result/action of ignorance. If one can root out ignorance through knowledge, where will, then, the body exist? The answer to these questions and doubts lies in this: The *Vedas* look at the *prarabdha* from outside, apparently. They do not look at it from the standpoint of a scholar. They only wanted to know if the body was the truth.

Brahma is basically a non-duality. It is complete in itself, without beginning, without end, axiomatic, defectless wealth, blissful wealth, eternal, always, true, inexhaustible, inherent in every thing, pervading on all sides, incapable of renouncing or accepting anything, has no bases, no supports, inert, subtle, desireless, self-proved, pure, enlightened, Himself, inaccessible to heart, mind, voice. Except Him nothing else exists.

"*Amarto-aham bhoktaamavikaroamvyayah |*
Shuddho bodhaswarupoahamakevalo ahamasadashivah | |"

According to this verse, "I alone am inert, non-consuming, defectless, indestructible, pure, in the nature of consciousness, only and Shiva. "This knowledge was imparted by Guru to Mahatma Apantaram, by him to Brahma, by Brahma to Dhorangiras and by him to Raikva and by him to Ram, and by Ram to all. This is the order for emancipation from the *Vedas*.

(3) *Shivasankalp Upnishad*

This *Upnishad* has only 6 *mantras*. Here it is exhorted that one's heart should have the determination to do good things only.

"O God! Sleeping or awake, our heart reaches far and near, and it shines in light like the stars. Make it one of noble determination. Fill and fix our heart with good intentions (*shiva-sankalp*). Such as the decisions of the *yogis* and great thinkers who perform *yajnas* and good deeds; this is the source of high knowledge; this, like a lamp, is self-lighted and light up and shine others; it has the power of memory; it has the knowledge of the past, present and future; like a divine *yajna* performer, it obliges us to perform the body *yajna* through senses; it is fixed like the axis of a chariot's wheels, contemplating of the *Rig*, the *Sam* and the *Yajur veda*; it is like a good charioteer who controls strong, fast running horses; this heart is the path-finder for scholars; it is located in the heart and is very strong and is not affected even by old age; it has very high speed; one does not know where it wanders. Such heart of mine, full of many unique attributes, O God! fill it with good intentions (*shiva-sankalp*)."

Fill heart with good thoughts, make it sensitive and free from defects.

(4) *Niralamb Upnishad*

This *Upnishad* deals with the nature and attributes of *Brahma*, and others such as God, Vishnu, the Sun, *Brahma*, the moon, *Yam* (the god of death), knowledge, ignorance, action, inaction, disciple, the fool, scholar, man, heaven, hell etc.

Brahma is the mightiest. Though he is inherent in ego, the earth, water, *Brahmanda*, action, knowledge etc., yet, remaining unaffected and untainted from all these things, He makes this Creation with the help of his *maya* and controls the mind of Brahma and other living beings by entering into them in a subtle form. In this form he is called *Parameshwar*, supreme. The experience of the physical (solid) in the form of *Brahma*, Vishnu etc. is called the *jeeva*. In other words, when Brahma as consciousness establishers himself as living power in different forms of being, He is called *jeeva*.

Soul is not caste, leather, skin, flesh, blood, or bones. To treat it as such is pure imagination. Likewise the work done with the help of senses is called *karma* or action. Performance of *yajna* or any *tapa* with an end result in mind is not action. The nature of *Brahma* is in what a man perceives him in all objects in this changing world. One can realize this through thinking and meditation, through restraint, and the service of a real *guru.*

It is stated that the persons pursuing the truth reside in heaven, whereas those lost in affections and greed of the worldly objects live in hell. Thoughts such as 'I am', 'I die', 'I am born' and other thoughts related to wealth, mother and father are figments of imagination, are the worldly bondages. Likewise the knowledge of such things as the desire for *siddhis* (realizations), *varnashram* order, fear, *jajnas*, fasts etc. is also bondage. On the contrary, contemplation of the eternal and ephemeral, and losing interest in the transitory world is called salvation.

That *guru* is worthy of worship, who helps you know and realize live *Brahma* in all objects. When one sees through one's ignorance of taking this world seriously and dwells upon the (knowledge of) deeper understanding of *Brahma*, then one becomes true disciple. A person knowing the soul in its knowledge form and yet performing his actions egoistically is a fool, an ignorant person, though he professes to be a scholar. One who performs *japa* and *tapa* with a view to get the splendour of Brahma, Vishnu etc. pains his inner soul. He is an extremist and his *tapa* has demonic overtones.

Efforts made to realize the glory of *Brahma* are *tapa*. The highest position is the position of *Brahma*. To consider the accessible world as true, accessed through heart and mind created by *maya*, is, in fact, inaccessibility. *Sanyasin* is one who tries to realize *Brahma.* 'I am *Brahma*', 'All this is *Brahma*'— he should be inspired with such thoughts and remain in a state of *Samadhi* without any kind of craving. He alone is respectable, *yogi*, *Paramahansa*, *avadhoot*. He alone is a Brahmin. Such persons are blessed by their *gurus* and are not re-born in this world. That is the secret of it all. They are emancipated, free from the cycle of birth and death.

(5) *Turiyateet Upnishad*

This *Upnishad* describes a conversation between Shree Adi Narayan and Shri Brahma. Revered Brahmaji gets to know the secrets of *avadhoot marg* (path of the rare men) from Shri Narayan.

Once the great old man Brahmaji met Adi Narayan and asked him what was the path of the *turiyateet avadhoot* Shri Adi Narayan, in reply, said:

"People traversing the path of *avadhoot* (unique) are rare. These people are highly learned, well-versed in the *Vedas* and see *Brahma* in every object. They set their heart on me and I reside in their innermost core of heart. They have four stages—*kutichak, bahudak, hans* and *param hans*. Through self-knowledge they know all the intricacies of knowledge. They give up *dand* (staff), *kamandalu* (a small vessel), *Kaupin* (loin-cloth) and other activities. They become *digambar* (completely naked) and become lawless (i.e. do not follow any rules and regulations) and do not wear even the barks of trees. They give up all kinds of worldly activities such as pasting a *tilak* on their forehead, hair cut, piety, sin, knowledge, ignorance and the *Vedic Karmakand* also. They give up hot or cold, respect, worship, pride, affection, greed, jealousy, desires, anger, happiness, pain, condemnation and disrespect, and see themselves as a dead body. As in the case of a cow, they go on living by taking whatever is available. For them, greed, scholarship, high and low are like dust. They give up all physical needs, and carry on their lives with whatever is available. They control their senses. They forget the *ashram-dharma* of life. They give up *varnashram* also. They are cautious, lonely and wander day and night like a mad man or ghost though they remain simple and unexcited like a child. They do not speak, keep quiet but go on contemplating their self and are constantly immersed in the feeling of 'Om'.

The sum and substance is that they give up all worldly and *vedic* activities. They are not afraid of the effect of any season. They give up everything. They see only *Brahma* and realize Him.

(6) *Subal Upnishad*

It has 16 sections, describing creation, how it was made, its creator and the cycle of birth and death.

First section. *Rishi Raikva* asked the great *Angiras Rishi* as to what was there before creation. How was the creation made? *Angiras* replied:

"Before creation there was neither *sat* (existence) nor *asat* (non-existence). In this situation, the first thing to be born was *tamas* i.e. ignorance. Then from *tamas, bhoot* (living beings) were born. From living beings was born the sky; from sky the wind; from wind the water; and from water the earth was born. This *Brahmand* (cosmos) changed into an egg. After spending one year in it Brahma divided it into two parts. The earth was formed from its lower half, and the sky from its upper half. Between these two a divine person was born. He had thousands of heads, eyes, legs and hands. This divine person created death first time for the living beings. Death had three eyes, three heads and three legs. It had a small *farsa* (sharp axe) in its hands. This divine person was *Brahm.* He entered into Brahma. This person created Brahma. Then this Brahma gave birth to seven sons from his mind. These seven sons of Brahmaji became *Prajapati.* Later on from this immense man the four *varnas* were born. Brahmin was the face of this immense man. King or *Kshatriya* was His arms; *Vaishya* were his *uru* (middle parts) and *Shudras* were born of his two legs. The wind was born from his ears, and *pran* (life) was born from His heart. All the fixed and moving things were born of Him."

Second Section: It deals with the formation of creation,

From the *apan* (rectal wind) were born *Nishad, Yaksha Gandharva* and demons. Mountains were formed by His bones. Medicines and vegetation were born from His skin cells. Rudra was born from the anger on his forehead. The breath of this immense man created the *Rig Veda*, the *Yajur-veda*, the *Sam-Veda*, the *Atharva-veda*, education, *aeons*, grammar, *nirukta*, stanza, astrology, jurisprudence, religious classics, critiques, lectures and episodes.

All the *loks* and souls live and find their place in Him, the *Hiranyam* (golden glowing) form. He divided Himself into two parts; half man and half woman. By Himself becoming a God, He created gods, and by becoming a *Rishi*, he created *Rishis*, and likewise He created *Yaksha Gandharva*, demons and the living beings living in forest and society.

At the end of Creation, that man burns everything to ashes in His *Vaishwanar* (fire) form. The whole earth is submerged in water and everything comes to an end and a situation is created which obtained before creation. This is the exhortation of emancipation, the teaching of the *Vedas*, and the discipline enjoined upon all.

Third Section: The form of soul element has been described in this section. Soul is without *pran* (life). It does not have a face or ear and does not hear; it does not have voice, brilliance, name, *gotra* head, hands or feet. Heart cannot know the limits of soul; it is eternal, limitless.

One can know, realise this indescribable *Brahma* i.e. should only through a six-part *Sadhana* of the truth, *tapa*, charity, farting, *brahmacharya* and impeccable detachment. Likewise one should observe restraint of one's senses, charity and compassion. Endowed with these attributes and resources, one who attains self-knowledge is freed from the cycle of birth and death and is absorbed in *Brahma* and himself becomes *Brahma*.

Fourth Section: This section describes heart (*hriday*), the place where the soul (*atma*) is located. In the centre of the heart is a mass of flesh of red colour. In this, that subtle element, *pran* (soul), grows and develops in many forms like the rare moon-lotus. There are ten holes in the chart where *pran* (soul) is lodged. When the soul element is placed there, it sees various scenes such as of towns and rivers. When it joins *vyan* (life giving wind), it sees gods and *Rishis*. When it joins *apan* (foul wind) it sees *yaksha*, *gandharva* and demons. Through *udan* (another wind) it sees the region of gods, and gods like *skanda* and *Jayant*. When joined with *saman*, it sees wealth etc., and when it is joined with *vaibhav* (grace and opulence), it sees the seen and heard of things of the past, the enjoyed and the unenjoyed, truth and untruth.

Heart has many nerves; and each nerve has seventy two branches. So, there are thousands of nerves where this soul, *pran* resides and acts through words. When it is in the second *kosh* (cell), then it sees and knows this world, the other world and all musical notes. It does not have any kind of desire when it is asleep. In that state, it does not have for company either gods, or their region, parents, friends and relations or the ignorant persons who are killing *Brahma* all the time. When it traverses the path of ignorance, it does not see anything except worldly affections.

Pran is in the nature of brilliance, immortality and nectar. It is a path, full of water and forests. Soul rushes through this route towards wakefulness.

Fifth Section: This section describes the location of soul in the body and its worship by different parts and organs of body.

Soul allows space to all who live with it. It moves through nerves, *pran*, science, joy, heart etc. This soul is *pran* itself. It does not grow old or suffer pain. It is not subjected to decay and death.

The ears of the soul make it hearable, *adhibhoot*. Directions are *adhi-dev*. Nerves are its central place. Soul pervades all words, directions, *pran*, joy and the cavity of heart. Therefore, knowing *pran*-soul, it should be worshipped.

Nose is the spirit. All the smellable objects are *adhibhoot*, and the earth is *adhidev*. Soul flows through all of them.

Tongue is the spirit. All the tasteworthy objects are *adhibhoot*, god *Varun*. Nerves are its central place. It senses/communicates through touch and the wind. That is soul.

Man, heart, is *adhibhoot*. Objects worth contemplating are *adhibhoot*. Moon is its presiding deity. Nerves are its central place. It moves in and through ego, egoistical actions and *Rudra*. This is soul.

Chitta, consciousness, is the spirit, thinking is *adhibhoot*; knower of the field is *adhidevata*. Nerves are its central place. The element permeating the nerves and knowing the field (world) is soul.

Voice is the spirit. Speaking-pronunciation is *adhibhoot*. Fire is its presiding deity. Nerves are its central place. It moves in and through voice, fire and nerves. This is soul.

Hand is the spirit. Taking is *adhibhoot* and Indra is its presiding deity. Nerves are its central place. This Indra moves the nerves. This is soul.

Feet are spirits, worthy destinations, *adhibhoot*. Presiding deity is Vishnu. Nerves are the central place. Feet, Vishnu permeate the nerves. They are present there, and are soul.

Genitals are the spirit. The action creating enjoyment is *adhibhoot*. Its presiding deity is *Prajapati*. Nerves are the central place. One which is permeating genitals, nerves, *pran*, science, joy, heart and the entire fixed and moving world is soul.

One should worship the soul element, *pran* permeating all the parts of body. Soul should be worshipped through all these parts of body because it is all, God of all inherent, is in the form of *mantra*, determination, pursuit of science which is the soul of time, and soul in the form of harmony of joy.

Sixth Section: Here the *Vedas* have been described in the form of Narayana. After narrating the formation of Creation, different parts of the body of (created) man, all gods, the *Vedas*, relatives and friends, nerves, the whole cosmos and the objects present in it have been described as (in the form of) Narayana.

He alone is the supreme immense Man (*Virat Purush*) of the past and future. He has eyes spread all over heaven. Only those persons can see and realize this status of Vishnu who have realized their own soul, *Brahma*. Persons who have given up their anger, and are alert all the times, can realize Him.

Narayana alone permeates every particle of Creation. He is the owner of this Creation and nurtures it. So, he can be realized through self-knowledge. He alone should be worshipped.

Seventh Section: This section describes the *Nitya Purush* (eternal God), the earth, water, air, consciousness power etc.

In a cave in this body besides one *Nitya Purush*. His body is this earth. He permeates the earth, but the earth does not know it. He permeates water also.

He is the inner soul of all living beings, a divine God, Narayana.

Elements such as water, air, sky, intelligence present in body are a part of God. Being ignorant, we do not know Him. But the aspirants, who through their *sadhana*, become informed and learned, know all these things, and realize that the divine knowledge is present in body itself.

Eighth Section: It describes the soul element.

In the depths of bodies of all persons resides soul. This body is filled with flesh and blood, and like a painted wall, like a town of *Gandharvas*, it is meaningless. It is meaningless like the inner parts of a beautiful banana tree and is fickle like a bubble of water. Though beautiful from outside, it has nothing inside, like the inner parts of the stem of a banana tree. Banana stem is not solid; it is spongy, delicate. But different from it, and residing inside it the soul has rare beauty, divine godliness; it is detached, pure, full of brilliance, formless, un-bodied and God of all. This resident of the cavity of heart is immortal and ever blazing.

In other words, this beautiful body reflects affections and *maya*, is lost in it. But the soul inside it is free from all this, and is divine and un-bodied. The wise and the intelligent try to discover and attain it; solid, physical body is available to all, but the knowledge of self, *Brahma*, can be attained by rare persons only.

Nineth Section: It describes how all objects, moving through the maze of existence, finally merge into *Brahma*.

Raikva asked Ghorangiras: 'What is the end of all beings and objects of this fixed and moving world? Where do they set finally?'

Angiras replied, 'Objects realized through eyes finally merge in the eyes; likewise tongue, nose, skin, voice, hands and feet, genitals (penis or vagina) intellect etc. finally set in themselves.

'Likewise, one inclined towards lifeless objects becomes lifeless himself. He is not born, He does not die. He doe not suffer pain. He is impregnable. He cannot be cut into pieces. He does not get angry, and only soul can burn or fire him. All this can be brought to an end only through the knowledge of the soul. One cannot attain or realize this soul through hundreds of lectures, study of the classics or through wisdom based on knowledge and intellect. It cannot be attained through the *Vedas*, severe penance or *tapa*, not through *Sankhya* (a school of philosophy), nor *yoga*, nor through the *Ashram* order; nor through any other means.

'Only the *Brahmagyanis*, coming out of lectures, admiration and *Samadhi* and those who listen to the knowledge related to soul can attain it. Only a quiet person, restraining his senses and aware of *Brahma*, discovers the soul in soul itself. His soul goes out, and he sees all things shrouded in soul. He sees himself in all things; he merges himself in all.

Tenth Section: It describes various *loks* and is written in question-answer form.

Raikva asked: 'Sir, what is *Rasatal* or the nether world replete with?'

Ghorangiras: 'With *Bhulok* (the earth).'

Raikva: And *Bhulok*?

Ghorangiras: 'With *Bhuwah lok.*'

Raikva: '*Bhuwah lok. . .*?'

Ghorangiras: '*Mahah lok.*'

Raikva: '*Satra lok*. . .?'

Ghorangiras: '*Prajapati Lok*. . .'

Raikva: '*Prajapatio*. . .?'

Ghorangiras: 'All *loks*, like beads in a string, are tied to and replete with *Brahma*, in soul form.'

In this way, one who sits pretty in the soul of these *loks*, merges in that soul. This is the way to emancipation. This the discipline and exhortation of the *Vedas*.

Eleventh Section: It describes the path through which soul exits body.

Raikva: 'Sir, kindly tell me through which path, and leaving behind which place, the rare soul comes out of body?'

Ghorangiras said that the soul element resides in the centre of the heart. In its centre there is a cell. It has four nerves. They are called *Rama, Arama, Ichchha* and *Apuna-arbhava*. Through piety, *Rama* goes to *Puunya-lok*. Through sins *Arama* takes it to *Paap-lok*. *Ichchha* makes one (soul) realize what has been desired, and *Apunarbhava* pierces through this cell. After piercing this cell, the soul pierces *sheersha kapal* (skull, head), then the earth, and then water, brilliance, air, heart (*mana*) sky, ego, greatness, nature, the undecaying and death. After that, piercing through *Param Dev* (Supreme God) it merges into it, because beyond Him is neither *sat* (truth, existence) nor *asat* (un-truth, non-existence) nor *sat-asat*. Thus the soul, piercing through various cells, finally merges with *Brahma*.

Twelfth Section: It describes a *sanyasin* who wants to attain salvation. How should that *sanyasin* conduct himself, and practise his *sadhana*?

Food grains were born out of Narayana. They were baked in *Brahma-lok*. *Sadhus* and *sanyasins* should take these food grains after remembering God. The food grains that they eat should be produced by them or begged by them. They should not beg from others. Instead, they should take food grains roots and fruits grown on independent places.

A *sanyasin*, therefore, should conduct himself according to rules narrated above. He should remember that food grains are born out of Narayana. A *sanyasin* should not beg it. Rather, he should take it from independent places. One will not realize Narayana just by saying, "Narayana, come to me." He will have to act. Narayana (*Shri Krishna*) has said in the *Geeta*, "Just perform your duty." A *sanyasin* should renounce all desires; then alone he can attain salvation.

Thirteenth Section: It is also devoted to *sanyasins*. A *sanyasin* should lead a simple and natural life, as in childhood. A child is completely unaware of worldly objects; a *sanyasin* should also conduct like a child; his conduct should be simple, detached and free from defects. He should sit in a *Samadhi* at a lonely place. He should consider all desires meaningless. He should not be afraid of living beings in the forest, like snake, tiger or demons. In other words, he should not be afraid of death. He should not be angry. Thus, like a child, a *sanyasin* should be innocent, unaware of the worldly affection etc. All his efforts should be directed towards the realization of *Brahma*.

Fourteenth Section: What are food grains? How is death identical with God? These issues are debated in this section.

The earth is said to be food grains. Water eats food grains. *Tej*, brilliance, is said to be the eater of food grains. *Tej* is food grains, the air is its eater. The sky is the food grains; the senses are its eaters. Senses are the good grains, *mana*, heart, is its eater. *Mana* is food grains; intellect is its eater. Intellect is food grains; the unexpressed is its eater. The unexpressed is food grains; the letter (which does not decay) is its eater. The letter is food grains; and death is its eater. In the end death finally merges in God, becomes one with it, .

Fifteenth Section: It describes how soul leaves the body. How and where do the five elements present in body disappear? How are they burnt up?

Raikva said, 'Sir when this scientific soul leaves the body, then who burns and which places?'

Ghorangiras replied, "When this scientific soul comes out of body, it burns *pran*, *apan*, *vyan*, *udan*, *saman*, *vairamya*, *mukh* (face), *pramachan*, *kumar*, *shyen*, *Krishna* and *nag*. After that they meet at their places. Then it burns the earth, water, *tej*, air and the sky. After that it burns the states of consciousness, dreams, sleep and *turiya*. Then it burns *mahat*, nature, the undecayed, and death. Death itself merges in God i.e. one after another, each one of them is burnt, and merged with its respective place."

Sixteenth Section: It describes the results of studying *Upnishad*. It is said that it should be taught to a deserving disciple only. Its reading and hearing blesses a person.

(7) *Mandal Brahmana Upnishad*

This *Upnishad* has five *Brahmanas* (books). The dialogue between great Muni Yagyavalkya and *Mandal Purush* is narrated her.

First Brahmana: Once the great Muni Yagyavalka reached *Suryalok* and said to him, "O Lord! Kindly exhort me about the soul element."

Surya Dev (Sun) said, "*Yam, Niyam* are called *ashtang yoga. Yam* are: cold, hot, control over food and sleep, always peace, fixity, control over senses. *Niyam* are: Devotion to *guru*, following the path of truth, to be contented in whatever is available, detachment, enjoying loneliness, control of heart and mind, renunciation and never craving for the fruits of action. *Pranayam* is the performance of *purak, kumbbhak* and *rechak*, 16, 64 and 32 respectively. *Pratyahar* means to control and withdraw heart from (the objects of) desire.

Samadhi is when you forget your *mana* (heart). These are the subtle parts of *yoga* and one who knows them frees himself. Five defects are: sex (desire), anger, indulgence, fear and sleep. These defects can be eradicated by determination, forgiveness, light food, fearlessness and through contemplation of basics. Sleep and fear are like a snake; violent ideas are like waves; strong desire is like vortex and women are like slush. In order to go across the ocean of the world, one should, crossing over even the virtues, take the help of the subtle path and concentrate on *Brahma*. One should, through practice, try to see *Brahma* between the eyebrows. *Sushumna* nerve, having the brilliance of the sun, is spread from *muladhar* to *brahmarandhra. Kundalini* is subtler than the stem of lotus, and is in the middle. All sins go away by seeing it once. When you close both of your ears by index fingers, then in the sound one hears one can see a blue flame in the middle of two eyes. The object/aim is that the aspirant has to become a *yogi* by seeing blue, black, red, yellow and a two-coloured mixed light respectively four, six, eight, ten and twelve-finger widths below the nose."

Second Brahmana: Yagyavalkya asked the *Purush* of *Aditya Mandal:* "*Antarlakshya* (the inner, main objective) has been described in many forms. But I do not understand it. What is it?"

Madal Purush relied: "A string of light of electricity is the cause of *panchbhutas*. In the middle of it there is a very deep and subtle light of the unexpressed element. You can know it by riding the boat of knowledge. This alone is the inner and outer aim. The world lies between them. One gets freedom by gaining their knowledge. First there is the *agni mandal*, and above it is *surya mandal*. Between them is nectar-filled *Chandra mandal*, and in its centre is the *tej mandal* of complete *Brahma*. This is *Sachchidanand Brahma*. One who knows it attains *Brahma* also.

Five states are wakefulness, dream, sleep, *turiya* and *turiyateet*. When *jeeva* (living being), in a wakeful state, is attached with and pursues desires then as a consequence he goes to hell. Due to wakeful state, I considered myself *tej swarup* (i.e. like *Brahma*) even in the state of dreams. After these two, in the state of sleep I considered myself *pragya* (one who knows everything) but now I feel that 'I am one' only. There were different states due to difference of place. But nothing is separated from me. Determination etc. are the bondages of mind. A mind free from determination leads to salvation. Once a man gives up his ego, and considers 'I am *Brahma*' and contemplates 'all are souls', he feels elated and grateful. A *yogi* in all respects becomes complete *Brahma*, beyond the state of *turiya*.

Third Brahmana: *Yagyavalkya* asked *Mandal Purush*, "O Master! I forgot the attributes of *manheenata* (dissolution of mind), which you narrated to me. Kindly repeat."

Mandal Purush, "O.K. *Manheenata* means separation of mind from soul, and merger of soul in *Paramatma*. This is the best state of an aspirant. To attain this state is called *manheenata*."

Fourth Brahmana: Yagyavalkya asked *Mandal Purush* the attributes of the five skies. He said, "The five *akash* (skies) are *akash, parakash, mahakash, Suryakash,* and *Paramakash*. *Akash* is dark both from inside and outside, *Parakash* is like the fire of death from inside and outside.

The element which has unlimited bright light both inside and outside is *mahaakash*. *Suryakash* is like the sun from outside and inside. *Paramakash* has indescribable light and a source of limitless happiness. One gets the same form or visage what one sees in them. A *yogi*, in fact, is that person who knows these five skies which have nine *chakras*, six bases, and three objectives.

Fifth Brahmana: It describes mind: "A mind devoted to objects of desire causes bondages, and one that does not indulge in them leads to freedom. So, all the world is an object of *chith* (consciousness). *Mana* (mind) is the cause of origin, existence and destruction of all the three *loks*. One who controls his mind reaches nearest to Vishnu. One realizes pure, undualistic, impregnable, complete element (God) before *mana* finally merges into God. This is supreme element. The whole world becomes pure on seeing it. By serving it even the most ignorant persons help in emancipating his hundreds of generations: His parents, wife, children etc.—everybody is emancipated."

(8) *Hans Upnishad*

Maharshi Sanat Kumar tells his disciple Gautam the secret knowledge of *yoga* in this *Upnishad*. *Yoga* has been described here through the medium of the knowledge of *Brahma*.

When Gautam insisted upon knowing about *Brahma*, Sanat Kumar said, "Gautam! Listen, I am telling you what Lord Shiva told Parvati after giving thought to various religions and opinions about them. This is highly secretive and should not be imparted to all and sundry. Just as there is fire in all wood, and oil in *til*, likewise this (the soul) is in all body, contemplating itself as 'Hans-Hans'. One who realizes it is victorious over death.

First of all, by drawing out the air from *adhar chakra* should be drawn out and one should go round *swadhishthan chaka* thrice. Then one should go into *manipurak chakra*, transgress into *anahat chakra*, take one's *pran* into *vishuddha chakra*, and holding it there, contemplate *agya chakra* and (in the end) *brahma-randhra*. While doing all this, the aspirant should think that he is *Om* himself. This will transform him into *Om*.

In this way one should contemplate of 'soul' residing in heart in the form of *Hans* (swan). Fire and *Soma* are the wings of this *Hans*. 'U' is its head, points are its eyes, face is Indra, both the legs are Indrani and time (death) is both of its hands. In this state, these feelings are in the control of *Hans*. One experiences *nad* (sound) by its countless recitals/repetitions. *Nads* are of ten varieties—*chini nad, chini-chini ghanta nad* (gong sound), *shankh nad* (conch sound), *tantra nad, venu-nad* (flute sound), *bheri nad* (drum sound), *mridanga nad* and *megha nad* (clouds' sound). Leaving the first nine behind, one should concentrate on the last, tenth. The practice of the first *nad* creates *chinchinahat* (a sensation) in the body. The second shows itself as if body is disintegrating. Third causes perspiration. Fourth leads to trembling of head. Fifth causes secretion of saliva from mouth. Sixth brings about the rainfall of *amrit* (nectar). From seventh you realize secret knowledge. From eighth you realize the sounds beyond (*para vani*). Nineth gives you the power to become invisible, and a pure divine sight. Tenth leads to the knowledge of *Param Brahma* (God) and proximity to Him. Once the heart is merged (in Him) all the desires and doubts disappear. One is freed from sins and piety, and the aspirant is lit up with all-pervasive, well-meaning, pure, eternal, unusually quiet *Brahma.*

(9) *Paingal Upnishad*

It has 3 chapters. Paingal reached Rishi Yagyavalkya and served him for 12 years. Then he asked him the secret of the knowledge of salvation (God). It is described here:

First Chapter: Creation is described here. In the beginning there was only *sat*. That alone is ever living, free from everything, having no defects, is in the form of truth, knowledge and happiness. It is everlasting, sole rare *Brahma*. He inheres the whole cosmos.

A special power, located in *Hiranyagarbha* creates an egoistic, *tamoguni* (of darkness) power, and in this *pradhan purush* (main power) is *Brahma* himself who nurtures and sustains creation. It is He who has dissolved into four parts the *rajogun* section of the *panch mahabhut* (five main elements), He created *pran* from the first three parts, and action senses (hands, feet and genitals) from the fourth part. Without the desire of Brahma all the gods and bodies remained lifeless. He wanted to make them alive and piercing through *Brahmanda* He entered into *brahma randhra*. That power is called soul. It is with this that the body could make a few efforts and was called *jeeva.*

Second Chapter: Paingal asked how the God who creates and destroys the entire creation become *jeeva*. Yagyavalkya replied that the physical body was made of five elements. Among them, skull, skin, bones, flesh and nails are a part (constituted) of the earth; blood, saliva, urine and sweat are a part of water; hunger, thirst, heat, affection, sex etc. are a part of the sky. Thus, all of them (elements) are parts of the body.

God took three parts of *rajogun* and created *pran*. There are five kinds of *pran*—*pran*, *apan*, *vyan*, *udan*, and *saman*. There are five *up* (sub) *pran*—*nag*, *kurma*, *kukar*, *Devdatt*, and *Dhananjay*. They are located in heart, nose and throat. From the sky, from the fourth part of *rajogun* were created action-senses. Voice, hands, feet and genitals are five action-senses. From the fourth part of *satogun* were created five senses— ears, skin, eyes, tongue and nose. *Vyashti* or a person comprises of 5 senses, 5 action senses, 5 *pran*, 5 *maha-bhoot*, 4 *antahkaran* (hearts), *kam* (desire, sex) action and ignorance. All of them perform their actions in the body and when this mortal body comes to an end in death, the soul goes out and merges in *Brahma*; and only *Brahma* remains.

Third Chapter: Here Paingal Rishi asked for dicta. Yagyavalkya replied, "*Tatvamasi*" (You are that); "*Tvam tadasi*" (You are that); "*Tvam Brahmasi*" (You are *Brahma*); "*Aham Brahmasmi*" (I am *Brahma*). These are four *dicta*. From the word '*tat*' we come to know the *sachchidanand* nature of unexpressed God, endowed with the traits of *maya* representing His omniscience. God being an object of innermost heart, we get to know our being different from Him in the word '*tvam*'.

In the same way the sentences '*tatvamasi*' and '*Aham Brahmasmi*' are heard. When one thinks about these sentences in loneliness, it is called contemplation. When one's mind is one and lost in *dhyeya* (object), forgetting himself and contemplation, then that state is like a lamp placed in an airless spot. This state is called *Samadhi*, and then the enlightened person comes face to face with *Brahma* and merges into it.

Fourth Chapter: Paingal asks what the activities of the knowledgeable persons are. What is their state of mind and being? On this Yagyavalka replied: "The heart of the informed persons proceeds by passing these paths, like an aeroplane. *Maharshis* say that once the soul is free from the senses, it really consumes and enjoys and God in person resides in such hearts. Therefore, this body is nothing. The wise should know *Brahma* in the form of knowledge. The activities of the wise are the service of the *gurus* and being immersed in the worship of *Brahma* only. A wise man may die in any circumstances, at any place, his soul finally merges with *Para Brahma*. The reason is that like the sky *Brahma* is present everywhere.

A person may stand on one leg and perform *Tapa* for a thousand years; he may not realize even one of the 16 *kalas* (varieties) of *Dhyan Yoga* (*Yoga* through contemplation). Even if he studies classics for a thousand years for attaining knowledge, he will not come to its end. Therefore, a man should understand well that *Akshar Brahma* alone is the truth. Life is fickle and mercurial; therefore eschewing the cobwebs of classics one should worship *Brahma* in His 'Truth' form. One should acknowledge that *Para Brahma* is present everywhere. If one does not consider oneself as *Brahma*, then it is like striking your fist in the sky or pounding the chaff of rice. This will not lead to salvation.

A man becomes holy like fire, air, the sun, *Brahma* and *Rudra* by studying this *Upnishad* daily. This bestows upon him the fruits of fasts, of studying the *Vedas* and taking a holy dip in the rivers in place of pilgrimage.

(10) Shatyayaniya Upnishad

It deals with the lifestyle of the four varieties of *Sanyasins* – *Kutichak, bahudak, hans* and *param-hans* and their *yoga sadhana*.

Salvation is required because there are bondages and *Mana*. *Amana* devoted to objects of pleasure is in bondage, and the one free from them is emancipated. If the intensity of man's involvement in pleasures is directed towards *Brahma*, he is bound to get salvation.

All the four varieties of *Sanyasins* wear the insignia of Vishnu, tuft of hair on head and *yagyopaveet* and worship regularly. The difference among them is due to their daily routine. None of them gives up signs. All perform five *yagnas*, know *Brahma* thoroughly. They give up the worldly *Brahma* and take resort to basics, roots (*Brahma*). They give up desires, *anger*, affections, honour-dishonour, and live in this world— emancipated. Though living in a body, they behave like bodiless persons. Bearing pains and pleasures, they wander in search of the soul. They accept alms, sometimes unasked just to keep the body and soul together.

A *sanyasin* should accept earthen and wooden vessels only. They should wear a dress made of straw or bark. They should get their heads shaved during transition of seasons. They should keep wandering, except during rains. They should live in a temple, cave or under a tree. They should have no desire except to see themselves in the form of *Brahma*.

The *Vedas* call that person a sinner who, though ostensibly a *sanyasin*, acts just in an opposite manner. One who follows the *Sanatan dharma* and rigorously observes rules conquers his senses, becomes pious, knows all the world, the *Vedanta*, *Brahma* and every knowable object. He attains *Brahma*.

(11) *Yagya Valkya Upnishad*

It presents a dialogue between Yogyavalkya and the Saint-King Janak regarding the *sanyas-dharma*.

On Janak's asking Yagyavalkya said, "After *Brahmacharya*, there is the *Grihasthaashram*, *Vanprastha* followed by *Sanyas ashram* in the end. But one can straightaway go to *sanyas* from *brahmacharya* or *grihasthaashram*. One may or may not have observed fasts, or been a scholar, served the fire; one can embrace *sanyas* with the growth of detachment. Then *prajapatya yajna* is performed. Or alternatively *agneya yajna* is performed.

One should perform *havan*, bringing fire from village. If fire is not available, *havan* can be performed in water. 'Water itself is god. I offer Him *havi*'. Reciting this *mantra* one should pronounces 'swaha'. Then taking some *hom* one should eat it. *Havi* offered along with ghee destroys diseases. The *mantra* for salvation should be read like this: 'That *Brahma* alone is worthy of worship.' Then plucking one's tuft of hair on head, one should pronounce thrice, "I have adopted *sanyas*." This is the procedure of adopting *sanyas*.

The hands, feet eyes and voice of a *sanyasin* should not wander. He should control his senses, and be a *Brahmachari*. He should consider and treat his body and his enemy one and the same. He should not be angry with those who speak ill of him, or harm him, because anger is the enemy of *dharma*, *artha*, *kam* and *moksha*. "O Anger, the destroyer of your own base! I *salute* you. My salutations to those also who imparted knowledge and detachment to me. When the world sleeps the wise is awake, and goes to sleep when the world wakes up. 'I am whole, everlasting consciousness, and this creation, too, is the same. A *yogi* should have this spirit."

(12) *Jabal Upnishad*

It comprises of dialogue between Brihaspati, Atri, Yagyavalkya and many *Brahmacharies*. It has seven sections:

First Section: Here Dev-guru *Brihaspati* and Rishi Yagyavalklya discuss *pran-vidya* (knowledge of lie). Brihaspati asked, "What is the region of gods? What is *dev yajan?* And what is *Brahma sadan* for all?"

Yagyavalkya replied, "The region of gods (*prans*) is where the un-freed live. This is the *dev yajan* of the senses, and is the *Brahma sadan* of living beings. One should consider it *dev yajan* and *Brahma sadan*. When *pran* (living element) escapes from body, *Rudra* exhorts the virtues and attributes of liberating Brahma, which leads to freedom and salvation. Therefore, one should worship *pran* in its unfreed state itself. One should not give it up."

Second Section: It describes the un-freed region in a dialogue between Atri Muni and Yagyavalkya. Atri asked, "How can we know this unexpressed and endless soul?"

Then Yagyavalkya said that he should worship the unfreed (soul). This soul is located in the unfreed. Where is the unfreed located? In reply to this, he said that it is located in the nerves. The nerves, which stop from committing wrong, also destroy the sins committed by them. The region where the eyebrows meet the nose is the place (also) where this world and the other (unknown) world meet. People with divine knowledge worship it in the morning and evening. Therefore, the unfreed is the proper object of worship.

Third Section: Here Yagyavalkya describes the path to salvation. He said that by repeating *shatrudriya* again and again one attains immortality (salvation). Man is, thus, freed from the cycle of birth and death.

(13) *Paramhans Upnishad*

Once Naradji expressed his curiosity regarding *paramhans sanyasins* before Brahmaji. This *Upnishad* deals with it. Only four *mantras* (verses) are there in it, Narad asked, "What is the vocation of *paramhans sanyasins*? What is the path they follow?"

Brahmaji replied, "The path of the *paramhans sanyasins* is the most difficult. So, they are rare. Once in a while you see a *paramhans*. They are highly pious souls. The leaned persons call them *Ved-Purush*. Their heart is always devoted to me, and I am amidst them. *Sanyasins* renounce their son, friends, wife and all actions performed after *yagyopaveet* studies, and even the whole cosmos. They carry only *dand* (staff), wear *kaupin* only just to cover their bodies. They use and wear these things for their bodies in order to do some good to others.

Along with these objects, they renounce heat and cold, pain and pleasure, honour and dishonour also. Those who renounce all desires, carry the *dand* of knowledge, and are lost in *Brahma* all the time are called *Dandi*. A *sanyasin* is a blot who entertains hopes and desires, does not have knowledge and is not detached, and begs alms. He is finally thrown into the worst hell, *Raurav*. One who knows this difference is *paramhans* (rare soul).

He neither blesses, salutes, praises nor criticises others or praises himself nor expects others to do it for him. He begs alms to fill his belly. He does not perform anything such as worship of gods, invocation, immersion, *mantras*, meditation etc. He does not consider other things or living beings separate from himself. He should not collect anything. Nothing is an impediment to him. For him nothing is worth seeing. A *sanyasin* who collects things is charged of assassination of *Brahma*. He is very far from beauty, joys, pain, pleasure, affection or jealousy. He rises above his senses and lives in his soul. He makes his life relevant and meaningful by believing and practising "I am the same *Brahma*."

(14) *Bhikshur Upnishad*

Different classes of *sanyasins* are described here. Mainly there are 4 kinds of *bhikshuks* (beggars) who desire salvation.

Kutichak: The *sanyasins* of this kind take only 8 morsels of food and attain *moksha* through the path of *yoga*. Gautam, Bharadway, Yagyavalkya, Vashishtha etc. were *Kutichak sanyasins*.

Bahudak: These *sanyasins* carry *tridand* (tripod like staff), *kamandalu* (a black vessel), tuft of hair on head, *janeu* and clothes of flame colours. Renouncing meat and good food, they take 8 morsels of food from a *Maharshi* and attain salvartion through the path of *yoga*.

Hans: The *sanyasins* of this kind do not stay in a village for more than one night, or in a city more than five nights, or in any region more than seven nights. They beg for food, and make efforts for salvation through *yoga*.

Paramhans: Such *sanyasins* eat only 8 morsels of food. They attain salvation through *yoga*. *Rishis* such as Samvartak, Aaruni, Shwetketu, Jadbharat, Dattatreya, Shukdev, Vam Dev etc. were *paramhans*. They live under trees, abandoned houses or in crematoria, and may or may not wear clothes. They have nothing to do with religion or irreligion, profit or loss, *varna* or caste. Seeing the same soul in all, they beg alms of all. They are clotheless, unperturbed, do not collect things, are lost in the contemplation of *Brahma*, and beg just to keep their body and soul together. Living in lonely houses, temple or on bank of river, near the holes of white ants, under the thatched shed of a potter, cave, pit or *yagnashala* they pursue *Brahma* through their pure heart, following the rules and regulations of a *paramhans*, give up the ghost.

(15) *Trishikh Brahmin Upnishad*

This *Upnishad* narrates a dialogue between *Trishikh* Brahmin and Lord Aditya, and details out various *asans*, indications/period to death and salvation. Trishik asked, "O Lord! What is body, *pran*, cause and soul?"

In reply Lord Aditya said that they should all be considered Shiva. He is everlasting, pure, *Niranjan*. Like a mass of molten iron, He transforms Himself into various forms. From Him have originated all things in this order: the unexpressed, and from it *Mahat* (immense, vast, great) and from *mahat ahankar* (ego) and from *ahankar* five *tanmatras*, from *tanmatras* the *panch mahabhoot* (five great elements) and from these five elements the universe was formed, i.e. the cause of all Creation is *Brahma*. He is spread all over, inherent in all things. This body is solid; *jeeva* himself is *Brahma*; he is (God) *paramatma*. Smeared in ego *paramatma* Shiva becomes *jeeva*. Ignorance and conjunction with nature makes *jeeva* engrossed in affections. Under the control and impact of passions, he takes birth in various forms of beings and wanders aimlessly like a fish, here and there. Death and time goad him to self-knowledge. Then he elevates and holds his *pran* in *murdha* (intellect) and practises *yoga* and attains knowledge from it. A *yogi* devoted to knowledge is never destroyed. In defects and play of passions he always sees Shiva. His 8-fold path of *yoga* leads him to higher and subtle stages.

There are two varieties each of *karma* and *gyan*. According to *karma-yoga*, a person, whose mind is unperturbed, becomes free form the bondages of desires. The steps of controlling mind, as spelt out in the *shastras* are *karma-yoga*. On the other hand, keeping one's mind always engaged in soul satisfaction is *gyan-yoga*. One has to attain a stage of desirelessness in mind in both kinds of *yogas* in order to attain salvation. There are ten rules for men: Non-violence, non-stealing, celibacy, truth, compassion, *arjav*, pardon, patience, meagre food and purity (cleanliness). There are 7 fasts; *Tapa, santosh* (satisfaction) charity, worship, listening to the *Vedanta*, sensitiveness (sense of shame) and recital (*japa*).

Asan: Different *asans* are as follows:

Placing the souls of both feet between thighs in sitting posture is *swastikasan*. Sitting with both heels tucked in back is *Gaumukh asan*. Putting one foot an right, and the other an left thigh is *Veerasan*. Sitting with right and left heels tucked along rectum is *Yogasan*. Placing the soles of both feet in thighs and sitting is *padmasan*. It eliminates all diseases and toxins. Sitting in *padmasan*, and holding the toe of left leg with right hand, and the toe of right leg with left hand is *Baddha Padmasan*.

Sitting in *padmasan*, and placing both hands on the ground, between knees and thighs and raising body above ground is *kukkutasan*. In *Kukkutasan*, tying both the shoulders with both arms and getting tied straight like a tortoise is *uttan kurmasan*. Holding both the toes of feet from being and drawing them close to ears is *Dhanurasan*. Pressing the joint from opposite sides with both heels and spreading knees and hands is *Singhasan* when you put both the soles of feet on joint between testicles and tie your hands, it is *Bhadrasan*. Sitting and pressing your joint with soles from opposite directions is *Muktasan*. Put both the palms of your hands on the ground and place your elbows to both sides of your navel; then lift your body up parallel to the ground. This is *Mayurasan*,

Matsyasan is formed when you catch the toe of the right foot with left hand, while the toe is placed at the base of left thigh. Put your left sole to your joint, and place the right foot on penis. Sitting straight in this posture is called *Siddhasan*. Spread your legs on the ground, catch their toes and press your head on to the knees. This is *Pashchimottasan*.

Sukhasan is that posture which offers you happiness and rest in sitting. Weak in body should start with this. An expertise in *asans* is like the victory over all the three *loks*. Once the nerves have been cleansed through *yam*, *niyam* and *asans* then one should start practice of *pranayam*. Human body is equal to ninety six fingers. *Pran* is twelve fingers above it. Once you measure the air in the body equal to it or a bit less through its (*pran's*) fire, you will attain the knowledge of *Brahma*. Body should be straight, erect in *asans*. Sight should concentrate on the top of the nose. Place your tongue up in the mouth and keep happy.

Method and Benefits of *Pranayam*

Pranayam means driving the air in four forms. Closing one nostril of the nose with right hand draw breath inside, there after holding it inside for some time, push it out from the other nostril. Likewise, practise it with both the nostrils, one at a time in opposite breaths. When you draw breath inside it is called *purak*, holding inside is *kumbhak* and drawing it out is *rechak*. In *Kumbhak* fill your body with air as a pitcher is filled with water. Thus the air is filled in the nerves and moves inside better. One's heart feels freshness, and you have a *darshan* of highly pure *Paramatma*. One should practise like this in the morning, noon, evening and at midnight.

Results: One day's practice of *pranayam* according to the above mentioned method redeems you of all sins. Its three-year practice gives you *yoga siddhi* (complete success in *yoga*). Such *yogi* conquers air and his senses. He eats less, sleeps less, and he becomes intelligent, prosperous, strong and brilliant. He lives long, and is spared untimely death.

In *pranayam*, beginning form small, slow breath to long deep breaths, you experience sweating, quaking and lifting above the ground respectively. *Adham* or the lowest *pranayam* frees you from sins and diseases, *madhyam* (medium) *pranayam* relieves you from chronic diseased sins, and *uttam* (the best) *pranayam* reduces faeces and urine. Body becomes light. In this state *yogi* is lifted above the ground and his food intake reduces. His senses and mind become sharp and he begins to know the past, the present and the future. Drawing breath through open mouth and tongue protruded in the early morning (*Brahma muhurta*) gives you *vak-siddhi* i.e. expert control on your voice and expression, and within 6 months you are relieved from chronic diseases.

Indications Prior to Death: This *Upnishad* details out the indications a man gets about impending death. They are like this.

When sensation is lost in the thumbs of hands, toes and feet a person dies in a year's time. On losing sensation in wrists and ankles, one dies in six months. One dies in 3 months' time after losing sensation in elbow. Loss of sensation in penis or vagina brings death in about a month. Losing sensation in eyes leads to death in 15 days; you die in 10 days on losing appetite. When your eyesight dims and becomes low like a firefly, you die in 5 days. If you do not see the tip of the tongue you die in 3 days, and if you do not see the flame, you die in 2 days.

Having known it, one should get busy in contemplation of God, recital of His name in one's own interest. Meditating on God one should make efforts to become one with him.

Once a man knows his soul (*jeevatma*) and God (*Paramatma*) and realizes 'I am *Brahma*', then the attainment of that state is called *Samadhi*. This leads to an end of all desires, and that *yogi* is not reborn in this world to practise *yoga*. He merges in *Brahma*. He attains salvation and reaches the region of liberated souls, *kaivalya dham*.

(16) *Advayatarak Upnishad*

This *Upnishad* describes the *sanyasins* and those aspirants who have successfully controlled their senses, and who rigorously adhere to qualities such as *sham* (repressing) and *dam* (controlling).

Brahma Rup: An aspirant is *Brahma rup* when he with full or half closed eyes, keeping his inner sight at upper brows, contemplates the brilliance of *Brahma* in *sachchidanand* form saying 'I am the rare consciousness of God.'

Tarak Brahma is one who drives away from the minds of

people the worldly fears such as those of conception, birth, old age death etc.

Tarak yoga has two methods—the first half and the second half. The first one is called tarak. Tarak yoga means that you see Brahma in all things, you realize Him in yourself and in all objects outside in the world, and you go on contemplating this form of Brahma. Its two methods are known as the visible and invisible also.

Advaya Tarak: Think that jeeva and God are enmeshed in maya whereas the rest are not like this (niti-neti). Now what remains after deducting the second from the first is advaya tarak. The kundalini strength in body is located in Brahmanadi sushumna in the centre of the spinal cord. It is spread from muladhar to Brahmarandhra. In the midst of it is kundalini having the brilliance of billions of lightnings. The yogis performor undertake their sadhna to awaken this strength of kundalini. One who realizes this strength attains salvation.

Guru: A guru is one who knows, and recognizes properly the holy souls, people endowed with and committed to yoga, people well versed in yoga, nimble persons, devotees of Lord Vishnu, people well versed in the Vedas, the real acharyas. 'G' stands for darkness, and 'Ru' means one who destroys darkness. That is why one who dispels ignorance is 'guru'. Guru is the highest, the ultimate resting place of man, paramgati, Paramvidya, Para Brahma, highest knowledge, and the noblest home to live in. As a preacher, he is the greatest among the great. You are emancipated from the world, just by pronouncing the word 'guru' once: All the sins of all the earlier lives are immediately destroyed.

(17) *Brihadaranyak Upnishad*

In size it is the biggest among all Upnishads. In its beginning 'Ashvamedha' has been explained. In describing various parts of the body of horse, a parallel with the form of the world has been drawn. Later on the unity of Brahma, Creation and Soul has been demonstrated.

The teaching of the divine has been imparted in the form of debate in this Upnishad. The first is the dialogue between Gargya and King Ajatshatru. Ajatshatru said that just as sparks from fire spread around in the same way living beings originate and emanate from Brahma. Brahma is the highest and the only truth.

The second famous debate is in the form of a dialogue between Yagyavalkya and his wife Maitriyi. She does not want to be rich, but is looking for ways and means to become immortal. *Maharshi* brought home the universality of *Brahma* through many examples.

The third debate takes place in the court assembly of King Janak. When the king offered to give a thousand cows to one who demonstrated himself as one who knew *Brahma* deeply and in subtle form, then Yagyaralkya satisfied the queries and doubts of one and all, and earned a thousand cows. Among the persons raising questions, the knowledge of Devi Gargi about *Brahma* was the most sound. She asked many questions regarding various periods and *loks*.

The fourth and the fifth debates were between Janak and Yogyavalkya. The *Rishi* comprehensively explained to the king the real nature and form of *Brahma*.

In the fifth chapter, *Prajapati* instructs all his three children—gods, men and demons.

In the sixth chapter are narrated both the stories from the fifth chapter of *Chhandogya Upnishad*. In the end of the Upnishad are the details of a *havan* required to be performed so that one acquires significance. Additionally, it is mentioned that one should take good food so that one may beget a brave, scholarly son of good moral character.

Upnishads Related to Krishna Yajurveda

Main *Upnishads* related to it are:

1. *Kath Upnishad*, 2. *Taittariya Upnishad*, 3. *Garbha Upnishad*, 4. *Akshaya Upnishad*, 5. *Skanda Upnishad*, 6. *Sarvasar Upnishad* 7. *Mantrak Upnishad*, 8. *Ekakshar Upnishad*, 9. *Brahma Upnishad*, 10. *Brahma-vidya Upnishad*, 11. *Yogatatva Upnishad*, 12. *Kath Rudra Upnishad*, 13. *Kaivalya Upnishad*, 14. *Panch Brahma Upnishad*, 15. *Sharirik Upnishad*, 16. *Avadhoot Upnishad*, 17. *Pran-Agnihotra Upnishad*, 18. *Yoga Kundalini Upnishad*, 19. *Dhyan-Bindu Upnishad*, 20. *Dakshinamurti Upnishad*, 21. *Kalagni Rudra Upnishad*, 22. *Rudra Hridaya Upnishad*, 23. *Saraswati Rahasya Upnishad*, 24. *Narayana Upnishad*, 25. *Chakshush Upnishad*, 26. *Kali Santaran Upnishad*, 27. *Kshurik Upnishad*, 28. *Shuk Rahasya Upnishad*, 29. *Amritnad Upnishad*, 30. *Shwetashvatar Upnishad*.

Shanti path or peace recital/invocation related to the *Upnishads* of *Krishna Yajurveda* goes like this:

"*Om sat navavatu| Sah nau bhunaktu| |*

Sah veeryam karvavahai| Tejasvi navadhi tamastu ma vidvishavahai| |"

i.e. "O God! Protect both of us (the disciple and the guru) together. Give to us together objects of consumption. We should undertake brave deeds together. Let our studies shine. Let us not be jealous."

(1) *Kath Upnishad*

This *Upnishad* was authored by *Kath*, the disciple of Rishi Vaishampayan. Therefore, it is called *Kath Upnishad*. It has two chapters which have 3 *vallies* (sub-divisions). It describes the discussion between Maharshi Udyalak's son Vajshrava and his son Nachiketa and Yam (God of Death).

First Chapter, the First *Valli*

Once Rishi Udyalok performed a *yajna* known as Vishwajeet and in the hope of getting the best results, he gave away everything in charity which included some such cows also which were very weak, old and incapable of bearing more calves. When his son Nachiketa saw this, he said, "O respected father! You have donated these old and weak cows. This is useless. It would have been better that you donated me instead."

Udyalak remained silent. But when Nachiketa repeated his statement, then Udyalak, in anger, said, "I donate you to death." On hearing this Nachiketa thought that the words of his father should not prove wrong. Therefore, he proceeded towards *Yamlok*, the region of the dead. When he did not meet *Yamraj* (the god of death), he waited for him for three days without taking any food or water. When *Yamraj* came to know this, he reached near him and apologizing said, "O Brahmin child! You had to wait for me for 3 days. So you can ask of me 3 boons dear to your heart, so that my mistake is atoned."

Nachiketa accepted this and asked:

First Boon: "O Lord of Death! When I go back home, my father should not be angry with me. He should become quiet and treat me well. We should all pass our lives happily."

Yamraj said, "O.K. It will be as you desire."

Second Boon: "O Lord of Death! Educate me with regard to the method and procedure of performance of a *yajna* to attain *swarg lok* (heaven), so that I also attain what is the status of gods."

Yamraj said, "Son! The knowledge leading to the attainment of heaven is like this. . ."

After this, *Yamraj* taught Nachiketa everything, beginning from the *yajna vedi*, method, *mantras* etc., and in order to test him, found out whatever was in his heart. Nachiketa repeated his desire exactly in the same old manner. On this, *Yamraj* said, "I bless you that the *agni vidya* I have taught you will be known as *Nachiketa Agni*. Take this string also, of varied beads and sounds. I give you this boon from my side. Whosoever worships this *agni* three times will receive knowledge from his mother, father and *guru* and will be redeemed of the cycle of birth and death. A man who actualizes/realizes this rare knowledge will gain the ultimate strength. One who learnt properly and worshipped the *Nachiketa Agni* three times will be freed from the bondages of sorrow and death, and will reach *heaven*."

Third Boon: "Lord of Death! The soul after leaving this body, assumes and accepts another body. Some persons acknowledge this, while others do not. What is the truth about this? Kindly enlighten me in this regard."

On hearing this, *Yamraj* asked him to go in for some other boon. He coaxed him as well. But Nachiketa stuck to his demand. *Yamraj* tested him in many ways, but Nachiketa said, "Sir, I want this boon only, and none other."

Second Valli: Seeing Nachiketa firm in his determination, Yamraj said, "A fool sunk in the greed of wealth does not appreciate or like the ways to attain heaven due to his indulgence and arrogance. There is no other world than the present one—the fools who believe in this die again and again i.e. are born and re-born in various forms of being.

"Soul is a part a spark of God. People have not heard about soul. And many who have heard, do not know the reality about it. It is a rare person who talks about it; and still rarer (unique) who realizes it."

"Even though you have thought about soul many times, you hardly know it comprehensively and well. You cannot know it through reason, but through the grace of an *acharya* who has realized it. God lives in this body, is present here. He reaches anywhere and everywhere, though sitting and living in this body. A sinner can neither see nor realize it. God lives in this body, but he is permanent in non-bodies. One who knows this Great Grace is never sad. A man of bad or loose character, practising no restraint and stuck up, cannot see it through subtle intelligence. Who can know the Great God who makes a food of living beings such as *Brahmins*, Kshatriyas etc. and a sub-food of death?"

Third Valli: "O Nachiketa! Only that person can understand the *pran tatva* (life element) who has controlled and overcome his senses, realized his soul and exercises discretion."

Second Chapter, First Valli

"O Nachiketa! Sovereign God has created the faces of senses towards outside. Therefore, they can accept and acknowledge only outward things. They cannot see the inner soul. A mindless person is ensnared in this outward show. But the learned man is not ensnared. The rising and setting of the sun is the cause of soul. One *Brahma* alone is spread everywhere. One who does not understand this, is lost in the cycle of birth and death; but one who realizes this attains salvation. Just as water, on mixing in water becomes like water, in the same way the soul element present in body merges (after death) in Him,

Brahma, the soul element i.e. the soul becomes one with Brahma."

Second Valli

"O Nachiketa! The body of God, in conscious form, has eleven doors or holes. One who knows this God becomes like Him, freed from sorrows, and freed from the cycle of birth and death. Therefore, a man who is not entrapped by the affections of these doors, reaches God. Living in different bodies and exercising control over them, it is God alone who assumes many forms. Therefore, one gets a reward in accordance with his actions. In other words, a man gets that kind of body in his next birth as he has deserved himself in this life through his actions. This Brahma acts according to the fruits of actions of this jeeva and accordingly the jeeva assumes form and status in his next birth." On hearing this Nachiketa thought to himself as to how to see and realize Para Brahma.

Yamraj understood his feelings and said, "Neither is this sun shining, nor the moon; neither stars twinkle by themselves nor the lightning blazes out. All of them are lit by His light. The whole universe is lit up by that Brahma."

Yamraj quenched and satisfied the curiosity of Nachiketa by imparting him this knowledge.

Third Valli

Roots downwards and branches going up, this perennial Brahma is like a peepal tree. He is consciousness; He is Brahma. He is called nectar also. Brahmalok finds shelter in Him i.e. the entire fixed and moving universe inheres Him. He is Paramatma. This knowledge about Paramatma leads to immortality. The sun and fire emanate heat due to His fear. The air, Indra and Death are active due to Him. To attain this knowledge about Parameshwar before death means salvation. Otherwise man goes through the maze of life and death. To break free from this bondage of death and to become Brahma means you have merged in Him, Paramatma. Nachiketa was freed from the bondages of death and became one with Brahma.

(2) Taittiriya Upnishad

It is the product of Taittiri Rishi. It has 3 vallies.

(i) First Valli: It has 12 dicta (anuwak) in which five great samhitas (collections) – 'Om', 'Bhuh', 'Bhuwah', 'Svah', and

'*Mahah*' – have been described.

First Dictum: Prayer has been made to *Mitra, Varun, Vishnu, Brahma, air* etc. for cooling off of three *taap* (fever) – spiritual, divine (*adhi-daivik*) and physical (*adhi-bhautik*).

Second Dictum: Significance of various chapters of education has been described. Consonants, vowels, *matras* (sounds), *sam* (understanding and cognition) *sandhi* (conjunctions) and *bal* (strength, effect) are the chapters of education.

Third Dictum: Five great *samhitas* are described here. '*Agni* (fire) is the prior, and *Aditya* (the Sun) is the latter form. Water is their *sandhi* (meeting point). Electricity is the conjoiner. This is the *Samhita* about *jyoti* (light).

'*Guru* is the prior and disciple the latter form, and knowledge is their *sandhi*.' This is *Vidya Samhita*.

'Mother is the prior and father the latter form. Progeny is *Sandhi* and the procreator is *sandhan* (conjoiner).' This is the *Samhita* related to progeny.

'Lower *hanu* (soul or awareness) is the prior and higher *hanu* the latter form. Voice is *sandhi* (meeting point) and tongue the *sandhan* or conjoiner'. This is the *samhita* related to soul.

'The Earth is the prior and *Dyulok* (the arena of light) the latter form and their *sandhi sthal* is space.' This is *Adhilok Samhita*.

Fourth Dictum: Appreciable '*Om*' of the *Vedas* is immense, vast, and of the nature of nectar. Indra should endow me with great mind. My body should glow and my voice be sweet— These are ominous sentences. Here Indra is worshipped.

Fifth Dictum: *Bhuh, Bhuyvah, Svahah* and *Mahah* are explained here. *Bhuh, Bhuvah* and *Svahah*—there three are *Mahalok* (great regions). *Bhu* is this earth. *Bhuvah* is space; *Svah* is heaven; *Mahah* is *Aditya*, the Sun.

Bhuh, Bhuvah, Svah and *Mahah* are fire, air, the sun and the moon respectively. Moon is the root of light. *Bhuh Bhurah, Svah* and *Mahah* are the *Rig-Veda*, the *Sam-veda*, the *Yajur-veda* and *Brahma* respectively. The *Vedas* are significant because of *Brahma*.

These four are respectively *pran, apan, vyan* and *anna* (food). Food itself is the *pran*-strength. These four have their four sub-divisions known as *vyahritis*. One, who knows them all, knows *Brahma* and receives divine grace.

Sixth Dictum: This *hiranyamaya purush* (*Brahma*) lives in the heart-sky. *Brahma* is like the sky. He is the truth, and give happiness to *pran* and *mana* (heart). He is indestructible. His worship leads to salvation.

Seventh Dictum: The earth, space, heaven, directions, sub-directions, fire, air, the sun etc. are *adhibhautik* (physical). *Pran, apan,* eyes etc. are spiritual. All of them are *prakrit*, nature-related, i.e. five elements.

Eighth Dictum: Significance of 'Om' is described here. 'Om' alone is *Brahma*, universe and creation. *Samgan* is also 'Om'. One studies the *shastras* reciting 'Om'. Nature begins with it. One knows *yajna* through it; this 'Om' orders *agnihotra.*

Ninth Dictum: It exhorts teaching and studies, and how to control one's senses. Satyavach, the son of Rishi Rathitar, considers truth the best, *Taponishtha Rishis* (*Rishis* undergoing severe penances) consider *tapa* the best and studious *Rishis* consider self-study the best of all.

Tenth Dictum: Rishi Trishanku says, "I pierce through the universe-tree. My glory is solid like rocks. Just as the sun has the power to produce greenery, likewise I, too, am nectar, liquid and the form of clouds." He said this in the same vein in which an enlightened person says, "*Aham Brahmasmi.*"

Eleventh Dictum: On completion of the studies of the *Vedas*, the *guru* exhorts the disciple, "speak the truth; follow *dharma*; do not be lazy in self-study; do not be lazy in the observance of truth, *dharma*, performance of the noble deeds, self-study, preachings and deeds dedicated to parents and gods; consider your mother, father and the guest as God. Follow the persons of good character. Wherever you are in doubt, follow the noble persons."

Twelfth Dictum: Here, too, as in the first dictum, prayers have been offered to gods.

(2) Brahmanand Valli

Five *koshas* of body are described here. It has nine dicta.

First dictum: A wise person carries out his *sadhana* in pursuit of God and attains Him. That *Brahma* is present in the sky and in the heart in body, those who come to realize this, enjoy the enjoyable things of life with *Brahma*. Sky was born of *Paramatma*. Later on air, fire, water, the earth, vegetations and medicines, man etc. were born. *Purush* has the element of food grains. The head of man is in the form of a bird. His arms are left and right wings. His soul is the middle part and his feet are the tail of this bird.

Second Dictum: It describes the significance of the element of food grains and explains *panchkoshas*. Living beings are born of food grains, grow with its help and finally merge into it. *Pranmaya atma* (Living soul) is not different in size than the *rasamaya deh* (vibrant body). Head is the *pran* of that soul, belch is its right wing and fart is left wing. Sky is the soul and the earth is its tails.

Third Dictum: *Pran* is described here. Gods, men, animals are active due to *pran*. *Pran* alone is age and soul. Body inheres soul and assume its shape and size. The *Yajurveda*, the *Rig-Veda* and the *Samveda* respectively are its head, right and left wings.

Fourth Dictum: *Manomaya kosh* is explained here. It is said that the knower of *Brahma* is never afraid. The soul located inside man (*Purush*) is *vigyanmaya* (scientific, subtle). The body itself is inherent in soul.

Fifth Dictum: This explains *vigyanmaya kosh*. Science extends action and *yajna*. Gods are worshippers of *Brahma* in scientific form. The soul inside the *vigyanmaya* body is *Brahma* itself, and gods also acknowledge this. Desire, happiness, indulgence, bliss and *Brahma* respectively are its head, right and left wings, middle body, tail and the abode of shelter.

Sixth Dictum: It describes *anandmaya kosh*. One who doubts the existence of *Brahma* is an evil person. One who knows the existence of *Brahma* is good man. God created the whole world and entered into it. Somebody saw Him in a form, and someone realized Him in a formless way. Scholars are of the opinion that the experience of God is the truth.

Seventh Dictum: Earlier the universe was in *asat* (untrue or non-existent) from. Then *sat* (truth or existence) was created. When it emanated from God, it was called *sukrit* (good action). God alone created everything. He makes efforts in this (activities of the world). One who knows this subtlety is a *Brahmagyani* and is emancipated. The ignorant meander through the maze of life and death.

Eighth Dictum: *Anand* (bliss) is explained here. A hundred blisses of man are equal to one bliss of a *Gandharva*. The bliss of man and *gandharva* is equal to the bliss of *Dev-gandharva*.

A hundred blisses of *pitras* (the dead), who have found a place in permanent *pitralok*, are equal to one bliss of *karma-devas*. A hundred blisses of *devas* (deities) are equal to one bliss of Indra. A hundred blisses of Indra are equal to one bliss of Brihaspati. A hundred blisses of Brihaspati are equal to one bliss of *Prajapati*, and a hundred blisses of *Prajapati* are equal to one bliss of *Brahma*. The one inherent in the sun and man is God alone. Those who are secure in this knowledge, renounce the world and realize *annamaya, pranmaya, manomaya, Vigyanmaya* and *anandmaya atma*.

Ninth Dictum: A learned man, who knows *Brahma* and how to break free from the bondage of sin and piety, does not depend upon anybody.

(3) Bhrigu Valli

Here Maharshi Varun clears the doubts of his son *Bhrigu* and asks him to realize *Brahma* through *sadhana*. This has 10 *dicta* and other things also.

First Dictum: *Bhrigu* requested his father to instruct him about *Brahma*, Varun said, "Food grains, *pran* (breath), eyes, ears, mind and voice they are all doors to go to *Brahma*. Living beings are born with them and live by them, and the place where the *prantatva* merges after death is *Brahma*." On hearing this, Bhrigu left for *tapa*.

Second Dictum: After *tapa* Bhrigu attains knowledge, realizes: Food grains are *Brahma*. In fact, living beings are born in it, live in it and finally merge in it. *Tapa* itself is *Brahma*. Bhrigu again started *tapa*.

Third Dictum: He realized: 'Acknowledge *pran*, as *Brahma*'. A man is born here and after death *pran* merges in *Brahma*. Knowing this, he resumed his *tapa* further.

Fourth Dictum: Now he realized '*Mana* is *Brahma*'. Living beings are born in it and finally merge in it. He again came to his father *Varun*. His father asked him to go back and resume his *tapa* further.

Fifth Dictum: This time he realized '*Vigyan*' (science) is *Brahma*. *Varun* sent him back for further *tapa*.

Sixth Dictum: He realized 'Bliss is *Brahma*. All are born in it, and finally merge in it.' Once this was determined, Bhrigu became *Brahma-gyani*, enlightened. The knowledge exhorted by Varun and realized by Bhrigu exists in the form of *param* *vyom* (the highest sky). One who knows it is enlightened, and is endowed with food grains, progeny, animals and good reputation.

Seventh Dictum: One should not condemn food grains because they are *pran*, and both body and *pran* depend upon it.

Eight Dictum: Do not be indifferent to food grains. Water itself is food grain. Water and glow are inherent in each other. Food grains are food grains i.e. food grains are produced from food grains and finally merge into them.

Ninth Dictum: Grow and increase food grains. The earth is the food grain. The earth and the sky are inter-dependent.

Tenth Dictum: A guest should not be disrespected. This is the principle pledge with regard to guests. Acknowledge him as God and offer hospitality. *Parameshwar* is present in voice, *pran* and *Brahmanda*. He exists in all in the form of soul.

One who considers *Parameshwar* as a shelter to all gets for himself the greatest shelter. One who worships Him treating as great becomes great himself. He considers God inherent in all things including food grains, and thus enlightens himself.

(3) Garbha *Upnishad*

This *Upnishad*, created by Rishi Pippalad, deals with conception (*garbh*) and the growth of embryo.

When the enjoyable desires rise in human body, then six *rasas* (*madhur*-sweet, *amla*-acidic, *katu*-bitter, *kashaya*-insipid, *lavan*-salty, *tikta*-irascible) are produced. They create a unique flow in body. Then from *rasa*, blood, flesh *meda*-muscles, nerves, bones, marrow and persons etc. are formed. These seven *dhatus* (elements) are formed in human body. Conception takes place with the sperm of man and ovum of woman. *Dhatus* or elements, placed in the heart, produce an inner fire. For some time bile at the place of fire, and air at the place of bile are what heart looks like.

During the period when conception is possible, after the establishment of pregnancy, the following stages are noted. It looks like *kalal* (a sound) in one night, *budbud* (a bubble) in seven nights, a *pind* (blob) in a fortnight, and in a month's time it grows hard. Head is formed in 2 months; feet in 3 months; knees, stomach and back in the fourth month; backbone in the fifth month; face, nose, eyes, ears etc. in the sixth month; life in the seventh month; and in the eighth month full body is formed. Excess of sperm (*shukra*) gives birth to à son; excess of *raja* (woman's orum cells) gives birth to a daughter; and when both are in equal number then an impotent (*napumsak*) child is born. A disabled child is born if the parents suffer from anxiety at the time of conception. Twins are born when the sperm is divided due to contact with air. In the ninth month, the embryo develops all senses. At this time it remembers its earlier birth and lives and its good and bad deeds appear before it.

Why Is Body Called Body?

The reason is that it contains three varieties of *agni* (fire). It has the *jatharagni*, the fire that helps in digestion of food, *darshanagni*, the fire that is visible; and *gyanagni*, the fire of knowledge, discrimination, which tells good from bad. Their places are fixed. *Ahvaniya agni* (fire of invocation), *garhapatya agni* (the fire for digestion) and *dakshinagni* (the fire of discretion) are respectively located in face, stomach and heart. Body, soul, *mana* (mind), senses, patience, head, skull, face etc. are *yajna*, *yajman*, *Brahma*, preachings for contentment, *havi* and *vedis* inside. Head is four skulls, and the line of teeth 16 skulls.

Constitution of Body: In the constitution of body there are 180 *sandhis* (joints), 107 *marmasthal* (sensitive points), 109 nerves, and 707 veins respectively. There are 500 marrows, 360 bones, and 4.5 crore cells. The weight of heart is only 8 *tolas* (*pal*), tongue 12 *tolas*, and the liver 1 *ser*. This quantity/ measurement is not fixed, because the intake of food determines the quality of faeces and urine, which are not the same in all men.

(4) Akshaya Upnishad

This *Upnishad* describes the questions and answers exchanged between Lord Sankriti and Lord Aditya. It has two chapters where *chakshu vidya* and *yoga vidya* are described.

In the first chapter Lord Sankriti prays to the Sun to remove the diseases of the eyes. In the second chapter all the seven stages of *bhog* (*asvidan* = non-sweating, *sushuptapad* = sleep, *asansarga* = untouched, *videhmukta* = not caring for body, *vichar* = thought, *swapna* = dream and *turya* = trance), through which *Brahma* is realized, are described.

(5) *Skanda Upnishad*

It describes *Brahma*, and both *Vishnu* and *Shiva* are treated as one and the same. Once a man turns his eyes inward and becomes introvert, he forgets his physical body and he begins to see *Hari*, only God all around: One who controls the minds and all fixed objects, and is in the form of knowledge, He is *Mahadev*; He is *Maha Hari*; He is *Parameshwar Brahma. Jeeva* is Shiva, and Shiva is *jeeva*. Shiva is Vishnu and Vishnu is Shiva. Both of them are in each other's hearts. Body and *jeeva* are only Shiva. With the dispelling of ignorance, one becomes pure and light. There is no difference between Shiva and Keshav. To see the absence of difference is real knowledge. *Brahma-gyani* begs alms only to keep his body and soul together. With the grace of *Nrasinghdev*, they treat Brahma, Vishnu and Shiva beyond thought, expression, and right as the epitome of the *Vedas, Brahma.*

(6) *Sarvasar Upnishad*

It describes various states such as those of bondage, emancipation, *vidya* = knowledge, *avidya* = non-knowledge, wakefulness, dream and *turiya* (trance) and family, *jeevatma, Paramatma* etc.

Bondage: The ego felt by *jeeva* in his body is bondage.

Emancipation: It lies in freedom from this bondage.

Vidya-avidya: *Avidya* is the cause of egoistic feeling. Its destruction is *vidya*.

Wakeful State: It comprises of cognition and acceptance of words etc. with the help of mind, intelligence, consciousness, ego and the ten senses.

State of Dream: It is when you are in a state of wakefulness, though you are not aware of sounds, words and other physical objects.

State of Sleep: When fourteen elements such as mind (*mana*) fall silent, and there is absence of specific knowledge and you are not accepting words or sounds, you are in a state of sleep.

Turiya State: When you are conscious of the origin and end of the above mentioned three states, you are in a *turiya* state.

The *kosh* formed from food grain is *annamaya kosh* and when fourteen winds pass through it, it becomes *pranmaya* kosh. When mind contemplates about the soul inside these two, it becomes *manomaya kosh*. When in the company of all these three, intelligence tries for knowledge and gets it, it becomes *vigyanmaya kosh*. The soul of all men is *Prabhu* (God) and witness to it is *Brahma*. He is neither body nor action. So there is no question of its birth or death. He pervades everywhere and is the soul of all.

(7) Mantrak Upnishad

It describes *mantras*. It is said that the students and worshippers recite them. Many persons, who are well versed in *Shastras* and the *Rig Veda*, worship *mantras* only. The secret of *mantra* is *Brahma*. These are located, placed in gods and demons such as *Kaal* (Time), *Pran* (Life), Death, *Sharva*, *Maheshwar* etc. They are in the form of *Prajapati*, Immense (*Virat*), and Water (*Jal*), and worthy of worship as in *Atharvaveda*. Some scholars call them 26th, and some 27th element.

(8) Ekakshar Upnishad

In this *Upnishad*, God has been assumed and explained in terms of a word.

O God! You are a word (undecaying). You are the sole protector of *Vishvagarbha Purana* (the most ancient from whose embryo the whole universe emanated), *parjanya* (those who are born to live and serve others only) and *bhuwans* (various spheres and *loks*). You are inherent in every particle of this universe, a shelter to poets, fire, father of the universe, the first born, *Hiranya-reta*, *yajna* and *Vibhu*. The life of the universe, births and various forms of beings are just your parts. You measured the whole cosmos by just one step. You are the cause and life of the whole universe. You are the Sun. In the form of *Kartikeya*, you are the commander of the army of gods. You alone are *dhata*, *vidhata* (legislating for all and nurturing them), air, *Garuda*, Vishnu, *Varah*, day and night, past and present and future, action, time and *param akshar* (the highest and the undecaying).

You are the light of the Sun, and the beautiful navel of the cosmic embryo felt in the throbs of heart. You are the God of all, protector of all spheres, the central base of all subjects, and *Prajapati* inherent in all. All the four *Vedas* sing paeans in your honour. You alone are woman, man, teen-aged boys and girls, *dhata*, Varun, king, rain, the Sun etc. You alone are *bhuh, bhuwah, svahah.* In other words, God resides in all.

(9) *Brahma Upnishad*

Omnipresence of *Brahma* (soul element) has been described in this *Upnishad.*

Navel, heart, throat and head—all these four organs of human body are those spots where *Brahma* is majestically ensconced. Brahma, Vishnu, Rudra and *Param Akshar Brahma* exist respectively with their effulgence during the states of wakefulness, sleep and *turiya. Brahma* is pervasive everywhere. Gods, *Rishis* and parents cannot tell us about Him. This *Brahma* can be known and experienced only through one's soul knowledge.

An aspirant of *Brahma,* giving up his *gyan-shikha* (tuft of hair on head) and *yagyopaveet* (the sacred thread) should wear the undecaying thread of search and knowledge. Those who have a fire within are the real wearers of *gyan shikha* and not those who made an outer show of it. Enlightened persons say that the true Brahmins are those persons who wear the tuft of (hair) of knowledge, and whose sacred thread is replete with *Brahma.* That is why the wise wearers of sacred thread are called *yajnarup* and *yajva.* God is the conscious state of all beings. He is inherent in all.

Just as a spider creates its own web and collects it back into itself, in the same way *jeevatma* moves from wakeful to dream state. God is so near and yet so far that man's mind and voice go far searching Him and return without finding Him. One who knows Him is emancipated. Soul is like butter in milk. It is not visible to anybody, yet it is there. But when milk passes through various processes, then butter and ghee come out.

In the same way a wise aspirant, through painstaking *sadhana* and *tapa,* realizes *Brahma* pervading his own soul.

(10) *Brahavidya Upnishad*

Devine knowledge is described in this *Upnishad.* Additionally the word 'Om' has also been explained.

Om (Aum): The divines have called in the word 'Om' *Brahma*—in one word, *pranav.* All the three main gods, three *Vedas,* three fires, and Shiva (comprising of three syllables) are inherent in it. The *pranav* sound is the essential condition of all living beings.

One should use *omkar* for peace, a word in which all words merge and the residue is *Brahma* alone. An intelligence totally engrossed in *Brahma* is called *amritkalpa*, i.e. one leading to immortality. *Jeeva*, being subtle like the hundredth part of the tip of a hair is *pran*. The contemplation of artless element located in the sky leads to freedom from the bondages of the world. That person is *hans* (rare swan) who recognizes the self revealed *chidanand* (God, in the form of conscious bliss) located in his heart in the form of unheard sound.

According to *Shruti*, the *Vedas*, *guru* (teacher) is the personified God. He is true always, everywhere. One who pronounces '*hans-hans*' is Brahma, Vishnu and Shiva himself.

Brahma, Vishnu, Rudra and Maheshwar hold their infallible, the highest place in the heart, throat, inner mouth, forehead and in the tip and beginning of nose. The *shastras* tell us that there is nothing beyond the highest seat/place of God. Twelve-finger width away from the tip of the nose exists the One beyond our bodies. The *yoga* of the *yogis* continue uninterrupted, irrespective of the fact as to where their eyes or hearts are. This is the most secretive and pure mystery. Considering *param akshar* (*Om*) everything, one should worship it, and carefully enjoy the knowledge-nectar of this secretive mystery.

On this earth the word '*Om*' is considered the best, leading to salvation and knowledge, being pure light and being unaffected from the sin of killing a Brahmin or the piety of performing *ashwamedha yajna*. It is an inspiring guide, it teaches informed, good conduct, leads to salvation, and presents before a men the nectar of knowledge of *param tatva*.

Om is the best sentence, the essence of the *Vedas*, *param Rudra, Param Brahma*, and is in all the gods. Gods have the rare light of *Om*.

The sun is present in the middle and navel of body. Fire lives in '*a*' and heart in '*u*'. Take *pran shakti* in '*m*' letter, present in the middle of eyebrows. In the 'a' of *Aum* is *Brahma-granthi* (gland) and in heart in '*u*' is *Vishnu-granthi*. In the middle of the eyebrows is *Rudra-granthi* which is pierced by the word-wind. In *akar, ukar* and *makar* reside Brahma, Vishnu and Rudra respectively. Beyond them is *paratpar*, the ultimate

God. Squeeze your throat and storm the strength of the merves. Press your tongue and move *kundalini*. Pierce the *pran* of *kundalini*, located in the most subtle nerve going to *Brahma-randhra* and moving upward to the eyebrows. Then you will hear a sound in *Brahma-sthan*. Then you will have a feeling of peace like immortality in your quiet nerves. Now one should light the lamp of knowledge by piercing the *shat-chakra mandal*, i.e. the cluster of 6 cycles. After that you will come face to face with God living in you, in all living beings. That God dispels all darkness and diseases covers you with knowledge. On having seen him, one should go on with the *japa* or recital of 'hans hans'. Body is called *pran* and *apan-granthi* is called *ajapa*. A man is transformed into 'I am the same *Brahma*' by reciting it 21,600 times daily. This is *Brahma-vidya* and this is the way to attain it.

The aspirant should always contemplate of *kundalini* in the east, and a *jyotirling* (shaft of light) in the middle of brows. Then he will be completely merged in *Brahma* and find himself pervading the entire cosmos.

(11) *Yogatatva Upnishad*

The significance of *yoga* element has been described here for the benefit of *yogis*. It is through a dialogue between Brahma and Shri Vishnu that the subject is explained.

Vishnu alone is the great *yogi*, great soul, and a great *tapasvi*, a dedicated person. *Purushottam bhagwan*, the Lord, the best among men, is like a lamp lighting the path of *yogatatva*. Once Brahma prayed to and requested Vishnu to tell him about *ashtang yoga*.

Then Shri Hari said that all the living beings were bound in the web of *maya*. The path of *yoga* which cuts across the *maya*-web takes you beyond birth, death, old age, and eliminates diseases, emancipates and helps you cross the ocean of the world, is like this. *Kaivalya*, salvation, is the highest post, achievement. It is very difficult to get. Even intelligence gets confused in the web of *shastras*. Since even gods cannot tell you about this highest post, then how will the *Vedas* help you.

Shri Vishnu went further and said, "I'll fell you the remedy to rid of all these defects. One who is devoid of *yoga* cannot have knowledge or salvation. One should be *mumukshu*, the aspirant, as well as one should practise *yoga* in a stead fast manner. Ignorance is the cause of our birth in this world; knowledge can free us from the cycle of birth and death, and lead to salvation. Therefore, the form of knowledge is the first and foremost requirement. The only means of achieving the *gyeya*, the knowable (i.e. God) is *gyan*, of knowledge. What is knowledge? Listen, knowledge is that means through which you know your own true nature as well as the creator of this world.

From practical point of view there are many variants in the *yoga*. But main among them are *mantra-yoga*, *hath-yoga*, *laya-yoga* and *Raj-yoga*. These four different forms of *yoga* are recognized all over. The four states of *yoga* are *arambh*, *ghat*, *parichaya* and *nishpathi.*"

It is further stated that Lord Vihnu alone is a great *yogi*, great *bhoot* (*prani*, living being) and *tapasvi* (dedicated). The wayfarer *yogi* of this *tatva marg* sees Lord Purushottam almost in person, like a beacon guiding him. So the *yogis* should recognize the importance of *yoga* and practise self contemplation through *yoga*. Once the 9 inlets/outlets are blocked, then the whole being becomes quiet, undisturbed and sees soul only as the residue. It is possible to realize this through the practice of *yoga*. Therefore a *yogi* should single-mindedly concentrate on the practice of yoga.

(12) *Kath Rudra Upnishad*

The knowledge of *Brahma* has been described here as a dialogue between *Brahma* and gods. Once gods reached Brahmaji and requested him to explain the divine knowledge to them.

Brahmaji said, "Cut your hair, tuft of hair, and give up your sacred thread. See your son and tell him—You are *Brahma*, *yajna*, *omkar*, *swaha*, *svadha*, *dhata* and *vidhata*. Then let your son say—I am *Brahma*. I am *yajna*. Then the *saryasin*, leaving his home behind and seeing his son and others should not shed tears. Progeny is destroyed if you shed tears. Then he should go round all *sanyasins* and move ahead in his mission. Such a *sanyasin* attains heaven.

This *tapasvi* finds himself pervasive in all, and sees himself in the hearts and minds of all. A *yogi* who has realized this supreme element goes beyond the limits of geography, history and time, and himself partakes the nature of God and becomes true *para Brahma*. Nectar-like, he does the welfare of all. The *Vedanta* describes seven attributes of every soul—*Brahma chuitanya, Jeeva chuitanya, pramata* (one who sets out to prove), *praman* (proof), *prameya* (the object of proof) and result. This differentiation is for purposes of convenience. *Brahma* is pure, conscious, without *maya* (illusion). Because of *maya, Brahma* becomes *Ishwar*, and due to ignorance He becomes *jeeva*. One who considers oneself relieved of ignorance realizes *Brahma*. This is divine knowledge.

(13) *Kaivalya Upnishad*

Param-pita Brahmaji exhorts Maharshi Ashvalayan, in this Upnishad, to gain knowledge of the real nature of soul, i.e. to reach *kaivalya pad*, the state of salvation. To reach/attain Mahadev is called equal to the realization of *Brahma*. The path lies through *bhakti-yoga*.

Brahmaji said, "One has to take help of faith, devotion, and *yoga* in order to attain the supreme element. He cannot be attained through action or wealth. You can realize Him through renunciation only. After ablution and bath etc. one should sit in a lonely place in a comfortable posture. Then contemplate his *guru* with full faith and think about his heart as lotus. Lord Shiva and subtle Brahma, who are beyond contemplation, can be realized by *munis* through meditation. He is all—Vishnu, fire, *pran*, the moon, the past, the present and the future. There is no other remedy for freedom from death, except His meditation. Therefore, one should realize *Brahma* by seeing all living beings in one's self, and oneself in all living beings. One who thinks and contemplates of Rudra becomes pure like fire. His sins of stealing gold, drinking wine and killing a Brahmin are washed away. He becomes pure, and thus attains the state of salvation."

(14) *Panch Brahma Upnishad*

This *Upnishad* presents a dialogue between Shalak, Pippalad and other *Rishis*, and Shiva is presented here as *Brahma*.

Once Shalak asked Pippalad, 'What was born in the beginning?' Then Pippalad replied, "*Saddyojat Brahma*". On asking, Pippalad described its two variants—*Aghor* and *Vam Dev. Aghor* is the inspiration of all gods, and administers the past and the future. These variants and characteristics should not be revealed to the underserving. *Saddyojat Brahma* is the supreme mysterious object of the world. Its boons are in the form of all kind of realizations. *Aghor* destroys all sins and evil persons, and offers glory and splendour.

Vam Dev is omnipotent and proffers knowledge. *Aghor* is supreme inspiration and witness to intelligence.

Through his *maya* Shiva keeps all glories in Himself and is without beginning or end. Even gods do not know Shiva properly, who is the *guru* of the whole world. None can stand Him, or before Him. Shiva reveals the world, and puts it into a harmony. He is *Brahma*. He is *Saddyojat Brahma*—it is said. He is *panchatmak*, i.e. ensconced in all five. I am that *Panch-Brahma*. This knowledge leads to salvation, and a taste of immortality. In the beginning of this *panchakshar mantra* *(Namah Shivay)* is the letter 'N'; and in its end is 'Y'. One should recite it. This is the true form of *Panch-Brahma*. One who studies this branch of knowledge of the supreme becomes like it and merges into it. This exhortation was made by Mahadev Shiva to Galav Rishi. Galav merged into it."

Therefore, the exercise of differentiation is based on ignorance. *Chaitanya Brahma* is the cause of all things. He pervades everywhere. Realise Shiva as an aspirant (the bestower of salvation) in all lotuses embodied in every cell of heart.

(15) *Sharirik Upnishad*

This *Upnishad* deals with human body, five main elements, senses etc.

This body is a combination of five great elements. This body comprises of the earth, liquid water, light generated by heat (fire), moving wind, and the empty part of the sky. Ear, nose etc. are senses for knowing. Ears, skin, eyes, tongue and nose have their bases in the sky, wind, light, water and the earth respectively. The senses of action are voice, hands, feet, rectum, and genitals. Their actions are speaking, taking, walking, discharge of faeces, and sexual intercourse. They are born of the elements like earth etc. The four inner hearts *(antahkaran)* are *mana* (heart), *buddhi* (intelligence), *ahamkar* (ego) and *chitta* (consciousness). Their objects are resolution, alternative, determination, pride and hypothesis. The spot of *mana, buddhi, ahamkar* and *chitta* are the end of throat, face, heart and navel respectively. Bones, skin, flesh, nerves, cells etc. relate to the wind; and desire, anger, affection etc. relate to the sky. Word, touch, appearance, taste (*rasa*) and smell – these are the characteristics of the earth. The first four are the characteristic words of water, the first three are of fire, the wind has two and the sky has one characteristic word only. There are three *gunas* (characteristics) – *satra, rajas* and *tamas*. Non-violence, truth, non-stealing, *brahmacharya*, non-anger, etc. are particularly the qualities of a *satvik* person. "I am the doer. I enjoy and consummate,"—this kind of pride reflects the characteristics of a *rajoguni* person. Sleep, laziness, theft, sex— are the signs of *tamoguna. Satva, rajas* and *tamas* are considered the best, medium and the lowest respectively. Not only this knowledge is *satvik*, knowledge of religion is *rajasik* and ignorance is *tamasik*. There are four states—wakefulness, dreams, sleep and *turiya* (trance). During wakefulness 14 senses are active—five senses of knowledge, five of action, and four *antahkaran*. In dream there are only four *antahkaran*, in sleep there is only *chitta*, and during *turiya* state there is soul only.

Mana, buddhi, ahamkar, the sky, air water and the earth— these are the vicar, off-shoots of nature.

(16) Avadhoot Upnishad

Avadhoot has been explained here.

Sankriti asked Lord Dattatreya, "Lord! Who is an *avadhoot*? What are his objectives? How do we recognize him?"

He replied, "An *avadhoot* is one who had become *avinashi, akshar*, i.e. indestructible; who has become respectable to all; who has freed himself of the bondages of the world, and who has the knowledge 'I am the same, *Brahma*.' One who has risen above the caste and creed, and settled in his soul, one who has gone beyond all divisions of high and low is *avadhoot*. *Brahma, mod* (joy), *pramod* (excessive joy) are his head, left and right hands. He is the very epitome of bliss and pure like a cow. A cowherd usually walks along the tail of a cow, and not its head, body or legs. In the same way God also resides in the tail of an *avadhoot*.

Avadhoots are great *yogis* who are sometimes wearing clothes, and sometimes not. They see the whole world full of *Brahma*. They are endowed with self knowledge and the knowledge of *Brahma*."

(17) *Pran Agnihotra Upnishad*

Taking body (*pran*) in the form of a *yajna*, it has been described along with its various activities.

According to a common conclusion of all the *Upnishads*, this body is a *yajna*. Once you know it, then you are free from the world, have attained salvation even if you have not performed *agnihotra* and are without the knowledge of *sankhya* (a school of philosophy). This *pran* i.e. the God settled in body is the *Brahma* pervading everywhere. Therefore, one who has comprehended body well has swum across the ocean of the world.

First of all prepare the *yajna-vedi*, contemplate all the parts of the body and then perform *yajna*. Offer *ahuti* to *pran* by bringing close and connecting thumb with the smallest (*kanishthika*) finger; *ahuti* to *apan* through *anamika* finger, to *vyan* through the middle finger, to *saman* through the index finger, and to *udan* through all the fingers. Keeping silent, offer one *ahuti* to *pran* and two *ahutis* to *apan*. Offer two *ahutis* in *dakshinagni* (southern fire), one in *garhapatya* (family) fire, and one in *prayashchitta* (repentant) fire. Take some water in your left hand, bring it close to your heart, and recite, 'Pran is fire. It is God. It is covered by five winds. It should make me free of the fear of all living beings. O *Pran*! You are like the universe; you are *Vaishvanar*, and are sustaining this Creation. For you this universe is like an *ahuti*.'

Thus, all the gods reside in body. A person, who performs *yajna*, reaches heaven after his death.

(18) *Yoga Kundalini Upnishad*

This *Upnishad* has 3 chapters in which are described the ways to awaken *kundalini* with the help of *pranayam*. Additionally, there is a description regarding *yoga* and *Khichri vidya*.

First Chapter: It describes various *asans* and different *pranayams* with the help of which a *yogi* awakens his *kundalini*, concentrates his mind, removes diseases of body and merges in *Brahma*. He pierces through six circles located in the body, reaches the lotus of a thousand petals, and attain salvation by reaching a states of divine bliss.

Second Chapter: It describes *khechri vidya*. One who is conversant with the knowledge of *khechri* becomes free from the travails of old age and death. Therefore, the old and diseased persons alone should practise it. It is impossible to attain this knowledge without instructions from a *guru*. It is a very rare discipline of knowledge.

A *yogi* acquires *khechri* strength through *khechri vidya*. In its practice, an aspirant conjoins *khechri* with *khechri*, and with the union of *khechri* seed transforms himself into a god and lives amidst them (gods). The symbol of *khecher* is syllable'H' (ह), of fire 'R' (र), of *dharana* 'I' (इ) and the symbol of water is 'M' (म). They make *hrim*, which is the seed mantra of *khechri*. This *mantra* helps in realizing the *khechri yoga*. The part of *Som chandrama* (moon) is 'S' (स). *Khechri* can be realized only through the exhortation of a *guru*, and after that the *khechri mantra* leads to successes in all fields. One, who recites this *mantra* 12 times daily, is not affected in his heart by the *maya* related to body. Five lakh recitals of this *mantra* carried out faithfully endow a person with its *siddhi*. The effect is that the wrinkles of face and body disappear, i.e. the old age is there no more. One should practise it only after careful understanding in order to avoid harms resulting from imperfect practice. If one does not attain *siddhi* even after regular and careful recital. one should consult his *guru* and proceed according to his advice. Once a proper understanding is made, then success and results follow in due course.

Third Chapter: According to this chapter, the real meaning of *pratipada* is the sun; of *purnima*, the moon; and *amavasya* means the obsence of both the sun as well as the moon. Desires lead to passions, and passions to desires. So, taking the help of God, one should give up both. In other words, one should free oneself with the help of self-knowledge. In the interest of one's welfare, one should give up base things and settle one's heart in the midst of strength. One can attain the highest state by scanning and examining one's heart in its own perspective. An intelligent and well informed person can be happy by penetrating and piercing through the six circles— *muladhar, svadhishthan, manipur, anahat, vishuddha* and *agyachakra*. That intelligent person acquires the knowledge of his own soul. Though living, he becomes as if un-bodied, and in the final analysis finds *Brahma* as the residue. This state of life is salvation.

(19) *Dhyan Bindu Upnishad*

As indicated by its name, this *Upnishad* deals with the art of meditation. Meditation is a part of *yoga.*

Innumerable and big sins, as big as the vast mountains can be washed with meditation. Beyond 'Om' the *beejakshar* ultimate point is *nad*, sound. When this *nad* merges in a harmonious manner into the *akshar*, indestructible, then what is found is the residue element, the wordless Highest Reality. A *yogi* attains salvation through acquiring a different word of *anahat* also. The subtlety of *brahma* element can be realised through meditation. God also pervades all things in the same way as scent in a flower, ghee in milk, oil in sesame, and gold in stones or beads in a string. God is quietly inherent in all living beings and all living beings, though not knowing, reside in Him. All the *yogis* contemplate Him for their salvation.

When *yogis* contemplate *Paramatma* (*atma*) present as a subtle light in a thousand-petalled lotus, they are rid of all sins. They pierce through six circles, awaken *kundalini* with the help of *yoga* and attain God.

Agachakra, located in the base of nose and between two eyebrows is the main source of the flow of *amrit*. The *yogis* realize it through their *yogic* element. This is *khechri vidya*. One should not, in ignorance, unilaterally practise it. It may harm. The guidance of a *guru* is a must. The *yogis* attain immortality through it.

(20) *Daklshinamurti Upnishad*

This *Upnishad* describes Lord Shiva, and analyses the Shiva element. *Dakshinamurti* is one of the names of Lord Shiva. When Shiva turns his face towards south to exhort knowledge and religion to the *Maharshis*, he is called Dakshinamurit.

Once many *Rishis* such as Shaunak reached Maharshi Markandeya, who lived a very long life, and asked, "O Lord! What is the secret of your long life? What is the source of your happiness?"

Then Maharshi Markandeya told tem that it was all due to his knowledge of the most deep, subtle and secret Shiva element. Shaunak Rishi asked again, "What is this highly secret supreme element—Shiva? Who is its god? What is its *mantra*? What is the source or method of acquiring it?"

Markandeya said, "That which helps you see Dakshinamukh

Shiva face to face is the knowledge of the most secret Highest Shiva element. The self-revealed and self-lighted god of this element's knowledge is the one who, at the time of destruction of this entire world, merges it in Himself and remain happy in the joy of his own soul."

"*Om namo bhagawate dakshinamurtaye mahyam megham prayachchha svaha.*"

One should recite this *mantra* and think, "This *Dakshinamurti* is pure like silver and a string of marble. His hands are curved in a *gyan mudra* and hold *amrit kalash* and a string of pearls. Snakes envelope His body, half moon is decorating this face and He has three eyes."

Later, the following mantra should be recited. This is a very special, and king of *mantras*.

"*Om namo bhagawate tubhyam vatamulvasine vagishas mahagyan dayine maryine namah.*"

While reciting this *mantra*, one should think of Dakshinamurti, the highest *guru*, who fulfils one's desires, who has beautiful hands holding gold, book, fire and snakes, whose face exudes happiness. He is wearing a free flowing garland. He wears a crown of the brightness of the moon; He destroys ignorance; He is *Adi Pruush*, the first Man, indescribable, the husband of *Bhawani*, and lives under a banyan tree.

The *mantras* mentioned here should not be considered separate from those related to *Brahma*, and should be recited with this knowledge to attain Shiva element. One should realize it in one's own soul in the light of devotion, emanating from the lamp of knowledge, filled with the oil of renunciation once ignorance is dispelled, this element reveals itself. One who studies and practises this discipline of knowledge is rid of all sins.

(21) *Kalagni Rudra Upnishad*

The dialogue between *Kalagni Rudra* and Sanat Kumar, along with the method of applying *tripunda* (a style of placing ashes on forehead) and its significance find a mention in this *Upnishad*.

Rudra describes it thus: "*Tripunda* is obtained from the ashes of *agnihotra* (*havan*). It should be taken with five *mantras* such as that of *saddyojat*. Later it should be charmed with the *mantra* of *agniriti* ashes etc. Later take it on your fingers with the *manastok mantra*, mix water in it reciting the *mantra* 'Ma no mahan'. Then place it on your head, forehead and chest chanting the *mantra* 'trayayush jamdagne.' Place it on your forehead in the shape of three horizontal lines, reciting *trayayush* and *trayambakam mantras*. This is called *shambhav* discipline (fast). On adopting it a man is freed from the cycle of birth and death, because this is Shiva; this is 'Om'; this is the Shiva element."

(22) *Rudra hridaya Upnishad*

In this *Upnishad, Brahma,* Vishnu and Mahesh are considered and described one and the same. They are one. This description is in the form of question and answer between Shukdev and Maharshi Vyas.

Once Shukdev came to his father and asked him to explain the position of Brahma, Vishnu and Mahesh (Rudra). Maharshi Vyas said, "Rudra (Shiva) is the soul of all gods. All gods are a part of Shiva. On his right side are the Sun, Brahma and three fires. On the left are Uma, Vishnu and the moon. All these three are one and the same. Uma is Vishnu, and Vishnu himself is the moon. Those who pay obeisance to Govind, who worship Vishnu faithfully, in essence worship Shiva. Those who are jealous of Shiva are jealous of Vishnu also. Those who do not know Rudra cannot know Keshav as well.

It is said that Rudra produces the seed, and Vishnu is the *beejyoni,* i.e. the vagina that holds that seed. Rudra himself is Brahma, and Brahma himself is the fire. Rudra takes Brahma and Vishnu in himself and the world partakes of the nature of fire and the moon. All men in this Creation are Shiva, and all women are Uma. One should know, realize *atma* (Vishnu), *Paramatma,* and *antaratma* (Brahma). Knowing all these three *atmas* one should seek shelter in *Paramatma* alone. The perennial soul of all living beings is Vishnu. All these three are like a tree whose branches spread upto the earth. Its top, middle and root parts are Vishnu, Brahma and Mahesh respectively. In this Vishnu is the action, Brahma the process of action and Mahesh is the cause of it. It is one deity which Mahesh has formed in three shapes for the activities of this universe. The world is Vishnu, *Dharma* is Rudra, and the knowledge Brahma. The wise *man* who recites the name of Rudra is reciting the name of all gods. Rudra is male and Uma female. Rudra is *Brahma* and Uma *Vani* (Saraswati). Rudra is Vishnu and Uma Lakshmi.

Therefore, the *jeevatma* is Shiva. He is the base root of the creations; He is its form; its action, process etc. The wise acquire this knowledge and become *Brahma-gyani*, and finally merge in that *Paramatma.*

(23) *Saraswati Rahasya Upnishad*

Goddess Saraswati's worship for gaining knowledge is described in this *Upnishad.* Maharshi Ashwalayan said that it was possible that man could attain the knowledge of *Brahma*, fulfil his heart's desire and gain intelligence by worshipping Saraswati. When you worship her, you cut across the illusion that is the world and its bondages, and you attain the status of *Param Brahma.*

A man aspiring to write poetry or desiring freedom from fear, or seeking fulfilment of desires and salvation, should worship Saraswati. Her worship destroys ego and pride, and man begins to realize *Paramatma.* All the weaknesses and bondages of heart fall apart, doubts are removed and a man enters into an ocean of joy in which he is rid of the results of actions. The person who realizes the imagined difference between *jeeva* and *Brahma* attains salvation.

(24) *Narayan Upnishad*

This *Upnishad* states that the creation originated from *Narayan.* He pervades the whole world in the form of soul. He is the past, present and the future. He himself is Brahma and Rudra. The word '*Omkar*' itself is Narayan. He is complete in Himself.

"*Om Namo Narayana*"

In this '*Om*' ॐ is a one-syllable (*ek ashar*) *mantra*, '*namo*' has two syllables, and there are five syllables in '*Narayana*'. This eight-syllabled *mantra* is an antidote to death. Besides, it bestows progeny, wealth etc. After that one gets immortality. One reaches *Vaikunthadham* (the abode of Vishnu) by reciting this *mantra.* It seems as if out of the effulgence of brilliance of heart the lotus has burst forth. Narayan, residing in all living beings, is the raison d'etre of their existence. He has no reason, or cause to explain Him. His study and worship in the morning destroys all sins of night, and worship in the evening destroys all the sins of the day. Thus the study of the aspirant makes him totally sinless. One should recite it in noon with face towards the sun. It will rid him of all the five great sins, and bestow upon him the fruits and benefits of studying the *Vedas* and the *Puranas.*

(25) *Chakshus Upnishad*

This *Upnishad* describes how to get rid of the disease of the eye. Worship of the Sun is mentioned in this context.

Chakshus Vidya or the knowledge about the eyes cures the diseases of the eyes and leads to realisation of God. Ahirbudhanya is the *Rishi* of this *Vidya, Gayatri* is its stanza, and the Sun its god.

This *Vidya* is like this:

Chakshu! Chakshu! Chakshu! Let my light be stable. Protect me, protect. Cure the diseases of the eyes quickly. Endow me with light. Improve and sharpen my eyesight. Do me good! Uproot, uproot all those evil deeds of the past lives which are impeding and blocking my eyesight. My obeisance to the Divine Sun who gives sight to our eyes. My obeisance to *Karunakar Amrit* (the Sun)! My obeisance to the bright Sun! My salutations to *Khechar* (the bright spot in the sky). My salutations to the great rajas, *tamas.* Take me from falsehood to truth. Lord Heat (Ushna or the Sun) is the epitome of purity and piety. Lord *Hans* (the Sun) is the other name of piety.

One who studies this *chakshumati* (good sense about eyes) daily does not suffer from the diseases of the eye. None is born eyeless in his family. You attain perfection in this discipline by making 8 Brahmins perfect in this line.

(26) *Kalisantaran Upnishad*

This *Upnishad* describes the ways and means to save oneself from the effects of *Kaliyug.*

At the end of *dwapar* period, once Devarshi Narad went to Brahmaji and said, "Lord! How will I stave myself off the effects of *Kaliyug* when I roam the earth. Kindly tell me the way-how."

Brahmaji said, "You have asked for a very good remedy. I am telling you the most deep secret of the *Vedas.* You will be able to free yourself from the *Kaliyugi* world by applying it. By pronouncing the name of primal man Narayan, all the sins of

Kaliyug will be redeemed."

Narad, "What name is that, my Lord?"

Brahmaji, "That name is '*Hare Ram Hare Ram, Ram Ram Hare Hare. Hare Krishna Hare Krishna, Krishna Krishna Hare Hare.*' These sixteen names wash all the filth of *Kaliyug*. There is no better remedy for the sins of *Kaliyug* than this in all the *Vedas*. These 16 arts destroy and dispel all ignorance of *jeeva*. *Brahma* is revealed to him, as the Sun is revealed when clouds disperse."

On asking for its procedure, Brahmaji said, "It has no method. You recite it in any state of body or mind, clean or unclean, you will feel proximity with *Brahma*, and will experience like becoming Him. If you recite it three and a half crore times, you will be rid of the sin of killing a Brahmin, a brave man or of stealing gold. The aspirant is rid (and becomes pure) of the evil deeds done towards one's forefathers, gods and other people. Sins end by abjuring all *dharmas* (i.e. rules, regulations and conduct), and one begets purity and piety."

(27) *Kshurik Upnishad*

Yoga-*siddhi*, i.e. success in *yoga* required for the deeper knowledge of basic elements is described in this *Upnishad*. Emphasis has been laid on the knowledge of *pranayam* in this regard.

Through *yoga*-*siddhi* a *yogi* can conquer death, i.e. he may free himself form the cycle of birth and death. Starting the exercise of *pranayam* slowly, the *yogi* should practise *purak*, *kumbhak* and *rechak*.

Later on, awakening *Kundalini*, he should pierce through *Brahma-randhra*, i.e. reach the state of *Brahma*. Then a *yogi* collects his nerves in the middle of his throat. Among them a hundred nerves are described as the best. *Sushumna* nerve is immersed in the supreme (element). *Biraja* is itself *Brahma*. *Pingala* is on the right and *Ira* on the left. *Brahmavetta* is one who knows thoroughly the space in between.

The pure edge of *yoga*, with the fire of *chhuri* (*kshuri*) or sharp knife, pierces through all the nerves of a patient, devoted person. Ploughing his mind with *tapa*, knowing all the wordless spots in different parts (of body), a *yogi*, conversant with *yoga*, cuts through all his bondages, and flies fearlessly in the sky like a swan. A lamp extinguishes after all the oil in it is burnt;

like that a *yogi*, too, burning all his actions, realises a harmony. '*Om*', the sharp edge of *pranayam*, rubs against the pallet of renunciation and cuts through all the bondages of desire, and a *yogi*, then, attains immortality.

(28) *Shuk Rahasya Upnishad*

The secret *Brahma Vidya* is explained here in the form of exhortation.

Maharshi Vyas said to Mahadev, "O Lord! Now the time has come when my son Shukdev should have the exhortation of *Brahma*." On this Shivaji said, "If I lecture to him on *Brahma*, then due to renunciation he would leave everything and would himself become light."

Vyasji said, "Whatever the consequences, my desire is that now he should have the knowledge of *Brahma* from you, become omniscient, and attain all the four kinds of *purusharthas* and salvation." Then Shivaji lectured to Shukdev about the knowledge of *Brahma*.

Shivaji said, "Instead of going on thinking about the meanings of *mahavakyas*, great sayings, for a hundred years, it is better that one should perform their *japa* along with the names of *Rishis* who said them. In this way, one gets better results.

"One element, the *Brahma* element, is found in all living beings whether they are gods, men, horses or animals. The pervasive *Brahma* element in the visible world is His own Light and is in the nature of soul."

All alert Shuk, on listening to this lecture, gave up everything and, immersed in the bliss of *Brahma*, went away to forests for performing *tapa*.

(29) *Amritnad Upnishad*

This *Upnishad* describes *pran upasana* and *yoga upasana*.

Just as gold purifies itself on heating, likewise through *pranayam* all the defects of senses are burnt away. It is prohibited that a *yogi* indulges in laziness, fear, sleep, food, anger and too much wakefulness or being totally foodless. Once a *yogi* practises daily in this method, then he certainly attains knowledge in 3 months, glimpse of God in 4 months, and salvation in 5 to 6 months. Along with knowledge and background of *panch mahabhoot*, the *yogi* should contemplate respectively on 5, 4, 3, 2 and 1 *matras* of *pranav*, and *pranav* itself. The place for *pran, apan, udan, vyan,* and *saman* is respectively in heart, rectum, throat, whole body and the navel. Their colour is respectively red like ruby, like *Indra-gopa mani, Dhusar*, the flame of fire, and the milk of cow. That aspirant or *yogi* attains *Brahma* whose *pran* pierces through all these circles and reaches *Brahma-randhra*. He is freed from the cycles of birth and death.

(30) *Shwetashvatar Upnishad*

Adi Shankaracharya has written a critique on this *Upnishad*. It is also significant like *Kaushitaki Upnishad*. This *Upnishad* tries to show the similarity between *Sankhya* and *Vedanta* philosophy. The secrets of the soul and *Brahma* are analysed clearly and the subject is rendered understandable by providing numerous examples. God has been visualised in a beautiful manner, e.g.

"*Tvam stree tvam pumanasi tvam kumar ut va kumari*|

Tvam jeerno danden vanchasi tvam jato bhavati vishvatomukhah| |

Ekodevah sarva bhuteshu gurhah sarvavyapi sarvabhutantaratma|

Karmadhyakshah sarvabhutadhivasah sakshi cheta kewalo nirgunashcha| |"

i.e. You are woman, You are man, You are youth, or maiden, and You become old and walk with the help of staff. You, on being born, assume many forms. You are one God living and situated in all living beings. You are That God who is omnipresent, the inner soul of all living beings, the master of actions, living in all living beings, witness to all, giving the consciousness and living element to all, you are pure and attributeless.

Primacy is accorded to Rudra and he is identified with *Paramatma*. It is said: *Eko hi Rudro dviteyay tasthuh.*

The first question in this *Upnishad* is: who is that *Brahma* who is the cause of the whole world? Who has produced us? Whose impact is keeping us alive? What is our base? Who is our Master?

Many reasons have been told in the *Vedas* regarding the origin of this universe. At some place TIME is called its reason, at other TEMPERAMENT is considered its cause. Are these the real cause of this universe?

The cause of this universe is *Prakriti*, nature. This *prakriti* is like the *nemi*, axle of a chariot. The axle has a ring of iron around it. In the same way, the three *gunas—satva*, *raja* and *tama*—surround this nature. The world is like a river. The river winds in a meandering manner. All this is illusion, and nothing else. This universe is situated in *Brahma*. He directs the universe. Man can attain immortality, on knowing this truth only. *Prakriti* and *jeeva* are the tendencies of that *Paramatma*, and He is the master of both. A person who knows this always remains happy. God is hidden in our hearts. The means of seeing that *Paramatma* is *Yoga-sadhan.*

Upnishads Related to Sam Veda

The main *Upnishads* related to *Sam Veda* are the following:
1. *Ken Upnishad*, 2. *Chhandogya Upnishad*, 3 *Vajrasuchik Upnishad*, 4. *Jabal Darshan Upnishad*, 5. *Jabalya Upnishad*, 6. *Maitreya Upnishad*, 7 *Kundik Upnishad*, 8 *Arunik Upnishad*, 9 *Sanyas Upnishad*, 10 *Yoga Chudamani Upnishad*, 11 *Mah Upnishad*, 12 *Rudraksha Jabal Upnishad*, 13 *Garuda Upnishad*, 14 *Savitri Upnishad*.

Let us examine what the *Upnishads* related to the *Sam Veda* have to say. Their invocation to peace is like this:

"Om apyayantu mamagani vakpranchakshuh shrotramatho
Balamindrayani cha savani sarvam brahmo panishadam maham

Brahma nirakuryam ma ma brahma nirakarot,
Anira karanam stvanira karanam meastu Tadatmani
Nirate ya upnishatsu dharmaste mayi santu, te mayi santu |
Om Shantih shantih shantih | "

i.e. 'May different parts of my body be strong, my eyes, nose, ears, *pran* and all other senses be strong. Let me not explain or expound *Brahma*, nor *Brahma* explain me. Thus, we should mutually not explain one another. I should imbibe the *dharma* which is inherent in *Upnishad*. I should imbibe that, and may all the three kinds of pains be relieved.

(1) *Ken Upnishad*

By 'Ken' we mean 'by whom'. Therefore, this *Upnishad* takes this name. It is mentioned in the ninth chapter, '*Talavakar Brahman*' of the *Sam Veda*. It has four sections.

First Section: In this *Upnishad* the spirit of *Brahma* has been described in the form of questions and answers between the disciple and the *guru*. The disciple expresses his curiosity in the form of questions. He asks his *guru*: who is that who inspires thoughts in mind?

The *guru* answers somewhat like this:

"Om Keneshitam patati peshitam manah ken pranah prathamah praiti yuktah |

Keneshitam vachamimam vadanti chakshuh shrotram ka u devo yunaikti | | "

i.e. He (God, *Brahma*) is the ear of ears, mind of the mind, voice of the voice, eye of the eye. He alone is the *pran* of *pranas*. A wise man who acquires this knowledge is rid of the cycle of birth and death. In other words, *Brahma* is all.

Disciple: "What or who makes *pran* the best?"

Guru: "The existence of whom makes mind think and contemplate is *Brahma*. In other words, mind gets inspiration from His promptings. But the names such as Indra, *Agni*, *Vayu*, Vishnu etc. with which we worship Him are not *Brahma*."

Disciple: "Who inspires the voice to speak out?"

Guru: "*Brahma* is the highest element of consciousness. He is voice, He is *pran*. It is His inspiration that makes the voice speak."

Disciple: "Who is it who makes eyes and ears function?"

Guru: "It is Brahma who endows eyes and ears with the attribute/property to see and hear."

Second Section: Here the *guru* teaches his disciple about the vast aspects of '*Brahma*'. He tells him, "If you think that you know God very well, you know Him in a very small form, small way. The form of God that you and other gods know is just a part (of Him) only. Therefore, '*Brahma*' is an object for you to consider."

On this, the disciple sat alone and for long and had a feeling that he knew God. He (disciple) further said, "Well, I do not consider that I know *Brahma* well; nor do I consider that I do not know Him. Therefore, I know Him and at the same time I do not know Him. Amongst us (disciples) one who harbours this thought in his heart that he knows and yet does not know *Brahma* is the real knower of *Brahma*. It is just proper that a man realises *Brahma* in one life time. But those who fail to know or realise Him in their life-time are born and re-born in various forms of beings in this mortal world. Those who realises Him attain immortality and are freed from the cycles of birth and death.

Third Section: It describes a dialogue between *Yaksha* and gods. In the fight between gods and demons, it was *Brahma* who in the form of gods defeated the demons. However, the gods ignorantly presumed that they defeated demons. So they became egoistic due to their victory. So *Brahma* decided to puncture their ego and appeared before them in the form of *Yaksha*. Indra asked *Agni* to find out who the *Yaksha* was.

Agni reached *Yaksha.*

Seeing him (*Agni*), Yaksha asked, "who are you?"

Agni: "I am *Agni.* My name is *Jatveda.*"

Yaksha: "O *Jatveda!* What power do you have in consonance with your name?"

Agni: "You see all these fixed and moving things upon this earth. I can burn them in an instant."

Yaksha: "O.K. Take this straw. Burn it."

But with all the efforts, *Agni* could not burn that straw and returned to Indra. Indra then sent *Vayu.* On seeing him, Yaksha asked, "who are you."

Vayu Dev replied, "I am *Vayu.* I am known as Matrishva also".

Yaksha: "O Vayu Dev! What power do you have?"

Vayu Dev: "Whatever exists on the earth can be blown away by me in an instant."

Yaksha: "Take this piece of straw. Blow it."

Vayu Dev could not blow away that piece of straw with all his strength. He returned to Indra and expressed his helplessness. Then gods requested Indra again to find out the truth behind it. Accepting their request, Indra himself set out to find out what was what. But as soon as Indra reached there, Yaksha disappeared. Indra reached Uma, the daughter of Himalayas.

Fourth Section: This section describes the *Brahma* element and its worship.

Indra expressed his curiosity before Uma Devi. Then Uma Devi explained to him that .he (Yaksha) was *Brahma.* Gods have acquired glory because of His co-operation. Then realisation dawned upon Indra. Agni, Vayu and Indra were the first among gods to know that Yaksha was Brahma Himself. And they touched (experienced) Him. Therefore, these three gods are considered the highest among gods. Indra is one who is born in the blinking of an eye or the flash of lightning. He is the godly form of *Brahma.* This is the exhortation regarding worship of *Brahma.*

Adhyatma Upasana Updesh: Mana (heart, *Brahma*) is called dynamic. Therefore *mana* remembers *Brahma* again and again. In other words *Brahma* (supreme) reminds you of *Brahma* (*mana*). *Brahma* is worthy of contemplation. *Mana* is there; therefore He should be worshipped with this name (*mana*).

Thus, one's ego is controlled, and divine knowledge leads to the knowledge of *Brahma*.

(2) *Chhandogya Upnishad*

It is a huge *Upnishad*, having 10 chapters, among which only the last 8 are in the form of *Chhandogya Upnishad*. In fact, this *Upnishad* is an elaborate form of *Chhandogya Brahman.*

First chapter has 13 sections, containing explanatory description of '*Omkar*'.

First Section: '*Om*' (ॐ) God should be worshipped in the form of this syllable. In this *Upnishad* it is sated that the base-essence of all fixed and moving living beings is the earth. The base-essence of the earth is water, the base-essence of water is the medicines dependent upon it. The base-essence of the medicines is human body receiving sustenance from it. The base essence of man is voice, his main part. The base-essence of voice is—*Richa* (verse). The base essence of *Richa* is *Sam*, and the base essence of *Sam* is '*Omkar*' (*udgeeth*). Therefore, *Omkar* itself is the best, supreme, *Para Brahma.*

Second Section: Gods and demons both are the children of *Prajapati.* But when they started fighting among themselves, then gods decided to worship '*Om*'. They worshipped '*Om*' with the strength of their smelling attribute. But the demons soiled and destroyed it. Therefore, it accepts both, the good as well as the foul smell. Then the gods started worshipping '*Om*' with voice. But this too was soiled and destroyed by demons. Therefore, voice is used for speaking ill and well. In this way, the demons took control of the eyes and mana (heart-mind). After that the gods worshipped *pran* in the form of '*Om*' (ॐ) The impact of this was that when the demons came to destroy it, they were splintered and destroyed like glass as soon as they collided with gods. They could not defeat *pran.* Therefore, *pran* is worthy of worship. Therefore, one should worship '*Om*' (*pran*) to save oneself from demonic and destructive powers.

Third Section: Here the worship of *Omkar* is described in godly form (*adhidevik roop*).

This heating Sun (*Aditya*) worships '*Om*'. When it rises it sings '*Om*'. It destroys fear in the form of darkness. The sun is virtuous like *pran.* When the sun sets, it is a sound. *Pran* is also a sound. So both are '*Om*'. They should be worshipped in this form. Therefore, a *yogi* should worship his soul in the form in which he sees it.

Fourth Section: This section describes the worship of '*Om*' in the form of a letter. '*Om*' itself is *udgeeth*. *Satvik* or virtuous gods, fearing *tamasi* (dark) death, entered into the *Vedas*. Therefore, all the stanzas (*chhands*) were called covering. The *Vedas* should be studied. '*Om*' and '*Brahma*' are one and the same. One who worships '*Om*' is rid of the fear of death.

Fifth Section: Here '*Om*' is described as *pranav*. *Udgeeth* is *pranav* i.e. '*Om*', and *pranav* is *udgeeth* (*Om*). *Aditya* too is *pranav*. Knowing this, the performer of a *yajna* corrects his mistakes with proper organisation of *pranav*.

Sixth Section: Here the earth is taken as *Rik* and *Agni* as Sam and worshipped. This earth is in the form of *Richa* (verse), and *Agni* is *Sam*. This *Agni* (fire) finds itself well organised on *Richa* (verse-earth). Singing of *Sam* is the godly worship of '*Om*'. Stars, sky etc. are like *Rik*, so they, too, are *Sam*.

Seventh Section: This section deals with spiritual worship, e.g. This voice is *Rik*, Sense of smell is *Sam*; the eyes are Rik, the Soul is *Sam*. *Som* is *Rik*, *mana* is *Sam*. The invisible man in the eye is the *Vedas*. He is the cause of all.

Eighth Section: It describes a dialogue between Shilak and Dalbhya *munis*. Shilak, the son of Rishi Sheelvam, Dalbhya, the son of Chikitayan, and Pravahan, the son of Jeebal—all these three *Rishis* were experts in singing *udgeeth* song. Once they started a discourse on knowledge.

Shilak: "What is the source of *udgeeth* (*Om*)?"
Dalbhya: "Sound"
Shilak: "And the source of sound?"
Dalbhya: "*Pran*"
Shilak: "And what is the base of *pran*?"
Dalbhya: "Food grains".
Shilak: "And the source of food grains?"
Dalbhya: "Water, without which foodgrains cannot grow."

In this way Dalbhya called heaven the source of water. About heaven he said, it is inaccessible. We take *Sam* as heaven, and worship him with that feeling.

Then Dalbhya asked: "What is the source of this world?"
Shilak: "The earth is the source of all. Therefore, it should not be trespassed. The earth is worshipped, and *Sam* is the base of the earth.

Ninth Section: In this section, *Pravahan* answers the questions of Shilak.

Shilak: "On whom does this world depend? Or seek shelter?"

Pravahan: "All the fixed and moving beings are born of the sky and finally merge into it. Therefore, this world depends upon the sky. God is greater than the living beings. Therefore, every body depends upon Him in all the three periods—the present, the past and the future. He is the best among the best and endless. Therefore, taking God in this form the worshippers of *udgeeth* continuously grow and reach the better worlds. In other words, *udgeeth* is the best and should be worshipped.

Tenth Section: Once there was a heavy hailstorm and rains, followed by a severe famine. At that time Rishi Ushasthi lived in a village of *mahavats* (drivers of elephants), with his wife under a very poor financial condition. One *mahavat* was eating *urad* (black gram). Ushasthi begged alms of him. Mahavat said that he did not have anything else than the *urad* he was eating.

The *Rishi* said, "O.K. Give me some from it."

Giving urad, *mahavat* said, "Eat them and drink some water."

The *Rishi* said, "If I drink water (from you) I will be guilty of taking your used (soiled) things."

Mahavat said, "*urad*, too, are used."

The *Rishi* said, "Well, if I did not get and eat *urad*, I could die, but water I can have somewhere else also."

Ushasti ate half of the *urads* and gave the other half to his wife. She had already taken a good meal. So she kept the *urads* aside for future. Next morning the *Rishi* said to his wife, "Well, if I get some food, I may go out and do something. Nearby a king is performing a *yajna*. There are chances, he may appoint me a *Ritvij*, the chief performing priest."

His wife gave him *urads* she had kept apart the previous day. After eating them, the Rishi reached the *yajna* site. There he said to *prastota* (presenter), *udgata* (main recitationist), and *Ritvij* respectively, "Well, if you worship a god without knowing, you will lose your head." On hearing this, every one stopped performing *yajna*.

Eleventh Section: Then the king asked the *Rishi* to give his introduction. The *Rishi* said that he was Ushasti, the son of Rishi Chakra.

The king said, "I know your fame. Initially, I looked for you, but when I could not find you I selected others. Now kindly help us in performing the *yajna* properly."

The *Rishi* said, "O.K. *Prastota* etc. should proceed with the *Yajna*. Kindly give me as much money as you would give to all other persons together."

The king agreed, *Prastota, Udgata* and *Ritvij*—all the three came to him. They said to him, "Well, you told us that if we worshipped a god without knowing him, we would lose our head. Kindly tell us who that god is?"

Ushasti said, "That god is *pran*. At the time of deluge, all merge into it. All living beings sing of *Aditya*. He is related to *udgeeth*. He is your God."

Twelfth Section: A divine *udgaan*, composed by Shvan, begins for food grains. *Shvan* means dog. But here it refers to one inspired with 'dynamism.' Once upon a time Bak, the son of Dalbha Rishi, and Rishi Glav, the son of Mitra, sat at a lonely place slightly away from a village for self-studies. Satisfied with their studies, a divine white dog (i.e. a Rishi in the form of a dog) appeared. Then many small dogs also gathered there and they said to the first dog: "We are hungry. So you sing *udgeeth* for food." The white dog asked them to come the next day.

On seeing this incident Bak and Glav also reached there the next day. The dogs held the tails of one another and went merrily around. Then they sat down, and using 'Him' *stobha* (a specific word of worship), they started singing *Sam gaan*. "O God, the protector of all. We desire to have food and water. *Paramatman*, You are a God of Light. You are Varun, the god who rains the desired things. You are the Prajapati who sustains all subjects, and you are Savita who has given birth to all. Therefore, kindly being food grains for us here. O the Master of foodgrains! Bring foodgrains here! *Parameshwar*, kindly make food grains available here."

Thirteenth Section. Here worship is related in terms of singing a song, as in music. Among 13 *stobhas* used in this context the word 'hau' indicates *manushya lok*, this world of human beings. 'Hai' is *vayulok*, the sphere of the winds, 'Ath' is *chandralok*, the moon-land. 'Ih' is the soul, and 'Ee' refers to fire. Additionally, 'Uu' refers to the sun, 'E' indicates invocation

'*Auhoyi*' is Vishvadeva. '*Him*' refers to Prajapati i.e. *Brahma*. '*Svar*' (sound) is a symbol of *pran*, life. '*Ya*' stands for foodgrains and '*Vak*' is the Immense. Thirteenth and the last *stobha* is '*Hum*'. He is the indescribable *Brahma*, inherent in all, and indestructible.

Voice itself presents its secrets before one who has known the mystery of *Sam*. Such a person gets all objects of his requirement, besides the capacity to use and enjoy them.

Second Chapter

This chapter has 24 sections.

First Section: Here *Sam* is worshipped in five and seven methods. It is stated that the *Sam* is the best in this world. In other words, all the fixed and moving objects of this world are *Sam*. So, they should be worshipped.

Second Section: There are five kinds of worship of *Sam* in different *loks*, worlds. Worship of *Sam* is performed through the medium of '*hinkar*', '*prastav*', '*udgeeth*', '*pratihar*' and '*nidhan*' respectively upon the earth fire, space, *Aditya* and heaven. In the higher regions (*loks*) also *Sam* is worshipped in this way. In the nether regions (*adholoks*) also there are five kinds of *Sam* worship. Here *hinkar*, *prastav*, *udgeeth*, *pratihar* and *nidhan* are called heaven, *Aditya*, space, fire and earth respectively. One who knows this deep secret of *Sam* uses and enjoys all things in the higher and nether regions.

Third Section: Rain is worshipped by fire methods. *Purovayu* is *hinkar*. The one that creates clouds is *prastav*. The fall of rain water is *udgeeth*. The flash of lightning is *pratihar*, and the stoppage of rains is *nidhan*.

Fourth Section: Worship *Sam* in all waters in 5 ways. Dense clouds, rains, eastward flowing rivers, westward flowing rivers and the ocean are *hinkar*, *prastav*, *udgeeth*, *pratihar* and *nidhan* respectively. One who worships *Sam* in water never dies of drowning or through water in any form.

Fifth Section:. Seasons should also be worshipped in five ways. *Basant* (spring), summer (*greeshm*), rain (*varsha*), *Shishir* (winter) and *Hemant* (autumn) are *hinkar*, *prastav*, *udgeeth*, *pratihar* and *nidhan* respectively. One who worships seasons in this way obtains the desired results.

Sixth Section: Worship of animals in 5 ways is described here. Goat, sheep, horse, cow and elephant are *hinkar*, *prastav*, *pratihar* and *nidhan* respectively. One who worships them in this manner is enriched by cattle wealth.

Seventh Section: Here the five methods of worship of senses leading one to the best life and divine regions are described.

Eighth Section: Seven-way worship is described here. Voice is worshipped in seven ways. 'Hum', 'pra', 'a', 'ut', 'prati', 'up' and 'ni',—the forms of word are *hinkar*, *prastav*, *om*, *udgeeth*, *pratihar*, *ubadrav* and *nidhan* respectively. One who worships voice is this manner gets the best voice.

Nineth Section: *Aditya* is *Sam* itself. In the sunrise, the Sun is *prastav*. At noon time the Sun is *udgeeth* and gods worship it. Later on the sun of the sunset is like *nidhan*. So, *sam* is *Aditya*. Worship *Aditya* is this manner.

Tenth Section: A seven-method worship of *Sam* is described here. It is thus worship of God. An aspirant worshipping in this way does not die premature, and conquers *Adityalok*.

Eleventh Section: Here *mana* is *hinkar*, Voice *prastav*, Eye *udgeeth*, ear *pratikar*, and nose *nidhan*. *Gayatri* is in *Sam pranas*. So, worship Him in the form of *Gayatri*. This worship makes the aspirant full of vigour. He lives a long, mature age, bright life, is bestowed with children, cattle, fame and a high state of mind.

Twelfth Section: Fire is worshipped here. Intense churning is *hinkar*, smoke *prastav*, burning *udgeeth*, ego *pratihar*, and the extinguishing of fire is *nidhan*. The aspirant of this *Sam agni* is brilliant, has long age, children, wealth etc. During the period of worship one should not sleep with his face towards fire, nor should one eat anything.

Thirteenth Section: Here it is stated that the couples, who worship *Vamdev Sam* while following the rules of married life, are endowed with good children.

Fourteenth Section: The rising sun is *hinkar*, the risen sun *prastav*, of mid-day *udgeeth*, of afternoon *pratihar* and the setting sun is *nidhan*. This great *Sam* resides in *Aditya*. Its worshipper has a glow, long age, fame and wealth.

Fifteenth Section: The movement of clouds, flash of lightning, falling of rain, thunder and the end of rains are *hinkar*, *prastav*, *udgeeth*, *pratihar* and *nidhan*. Its worshipper is endowed with children, cattle wealth etc.

Sixteenth Section: Here, among seasons, the worship

described is one of *Vairaj Sam*. Its worshipper is gifted with a glow and cattle wealth; therefore, one should not condemn seasons.

Seventeenth Section: Here the worshipper assumes that *Shakvari Sam* is found in all worlds, and therefore worships *Sam*. He gets all the good things of the world.

Eighteenth Section: Worship is advised on the assumption of Agriculture (*Krisi*) *Sam*. Its devotee gets cattle and farming wealth.

Nineteenth Section: In this section the worship advocated is of *Yajnayajniya Sam*. It is assumed that *yajna* does not have any parts or organs. Its worshipper has fully developed parts or organs and is endowed with children, cattle and wealth.

Twentieth Section: Worship of *Rajan Sam* is described here. Its worshipper attains *Dev Lok*, *Rishi Lok* and proximity to and company of God.

Twenty-First Section: *Trayi Vidya* or the knowledge of the *Vedas* is *hinkar*; all the three *Loks*—*prastav*, *Agni*, *Vayu*, and *Aditya* are *udgeeth*, stars, rays and birds are *pratihar*, and sarva, gandharva and pitar are *nidhan*. He is present in all. One who worships assuming the group of *Sam* in this knowledge of intelligence immerses himself in all i.e. he becomes God himself.

Twenty-Second Section: Here the worship of Indra is described, assuming that he is the soul of all sounds. In addition to it the significance of *agni-gan*, *vayu-gan* and *Indra-gan* is also highlighted. The tone of these sounds should be loud and pronounced vigorously. But the touching or connecting letters should be pronounced slowly and clearly, and at that time, one should think that death is going out of body.

Twenty-Third Section: *Yajna*, studies and action—these are three parts of actions which lead to piety, fame and freedom. Prajapati had a feeling, realised that the *Vedas* are the essence of the world. When he gave more thought, he realised 'bhuh', 'bhuwah', and 'svah'. After acknowledging the essence of all three (*Vedas*), he had a feeling of 'Om'. This is *Brahma*. He inheres all living beings. He is *Paramatma*.

Twenty-Fourth Section: As per the followers of *Brahma-vad*, morning, noon and evening are the times for *yajna*, as they are the times of *Vasus*, *Rudras* and *Adityas* respectively. The performer of *yajna* should have a knowledge of these times. That performer of *yajna* is ignorant who does not have proper knowledge of time of the *yajman lok*.

The *yajna* should be performed (executed) by only that person who knows time. In the morning, before the recitation of *Richas*, the *yajman* (the person who wants the *yajna* to be performed for him) should sing of '*vasudev*' with his face towards north. 'O *Agni!* Open your doors, so that we can see you for acquiring kingdom.' Then after saluting fire and saying 'I will reach the *yajman lok* and will come here after death' he should perform *havan*. In the same way the *yajman* should sing in praise of the wind and *Aditya* located in space. Then he gets the desired results.

Third Chapter

It has nineteen sections where the worship of the Sun in the form of honey, and five *pranas* is described.

First to Fifth Section: Here the Sun is worshipped as honey. It is called *Madhu Vidya* also. Its rays in the east are like *Richas*, the *Rig-Veda* and the *Sam Veda*. They are the holes in the honeycomb, honeybees, flowers and their nectar-like *rasa* respectively. Its rays in the south are the *Yajur-veda*, the *mantras* of the '*Yajur-veda*' and Soma is the nectar-like water. Its rays in the west are the *Sam-veda*, the *mantras* of the *Sam-veda*, Soma etc. The Sun sustains the whole universe and gives life to it. We should worship the Sun.

Sixth to Eleventh Section: The *Madhu Vidya* narrated in the above sections is detailed here from sixth to tenth section. The honey or *rasa* is described. Gods, *vasuganas*, *marudganas*, and *sadhyaganas* remain fully filled and satisfied with this nectar-like *rasa*, without eating anything else. This flow of nectar comes from the Sun, keeps them satisfied and they realise the nature of God. In the eleventh section it is said that on being merged in *Brahma*, the living beings neither rise nor set. They are ensconced in their rare glow. In *Brahmalok* there is neither the sunrise nor the sunset. One who knows this secret, finds sun-light all the time. This *Madhu vidya* was realised/attained by *Hiranyagarbha*, Virat, Manu, Prajapati, Arupa and Udyalok Muni. This secret knowledge should be imparted by father to his eldest son, or by a *guru* to his most able disciple and to none else.

Twelfth Section: *Gayatri* is situated to be present all over, in this section.

Presentation of Gayatri: All living beings are of the nature of *Gayatri*. All fixed and moving things are *Gayatri*. Voice, the Earth and *Pran*—they all are *Gayatri*. *Gayatri* has four stages and six kinds. Its *mantra* is:

"Om bhurbhuvah svah tatsaviturvarenyam
bhargo devasya dhimahi
dhiyo yonah prachodayat I"

Brahma in *Gayatri* form is supremely significant. One step (or stage) of this *Brahma* is all the living beings. This pre-eminent *Brahma* in the form of *Purush* (i.e. Supreme power) is present outside the sky, inside the sky, and in the sky located in the lotus-heart of human beings. The worshipper of this whole and indestructible *Brahma* finally and completely merges in Him.

Thirteenth Section: It contains description related to the worship of *Gayatri*.

Five Pranas of Gayatri Worship: There are five doors in human body, protected by the gods. They are: the eastern hole—*pran*, eyes, *Aditya*, glow and foodgrains etc. Southern hole is *vyan*, ears, the moon, glory and fame.Western hole consists of *apan*, voice and fire. Northern hole is *saman*, *mana*, cloud, fame and individual (beauty of body). Upper hole is *udan*, air, the sky and the glow. One who knows them all worships them and, in return, gains fame and glory, highly aroused appelite, beauty born of performing *yajna*, and greatness combined with strength, respectively. These five purush ensconced in heart are various forms of God and are the doormen of heaven. Their worshipper is blessed with brave children in his family who realise God.

Fourteenth Section: Worship of God in visual or physical form is described here.

Sagunopasana: *Brahma* is pervasive in all fixed and moving beings and inheres them. The whole universe is born of *Brahma* and finally merges into Him. Therefore, one should try to gain knowledge of *Brahma*.

Fifteenth Section: Just as space never gets old or is worn out, likewise *Brahma* too is never worn out. Therefore, seek His shelter and traverse the path of His realisation.

Sixteenth Section: It describes the worship of *pran*:

Worship of pran for a long life: *Purush* (man) is *yajna*.

His (of his age) 24 years are *pratahsavan* (morning or the first stage). He is related to *Gayatri*. *Gayatri*, too, has 24 letters in it. *Pranas* are *Vasus*, because they create all living beings. People who are unhappy or suffering in this age should pray: "O *Pranas* in the form *Vasus*! Identify my morning stage with midday *(madhyandin) yajna*, so that I am not separated from *Vasus*." Later on 44 years of man's life are midday *yajna*. They are related to *trishtup chhanda* (stanza). *Trishtup* has 44 letters in it. *Rudras* are in it. *Pran* is *Rudra*, because He makes all weep. In this stage recite this *mantra* for relief from sufferings, "O Rudras in the form of Pranas! Merge it into the third stage, so that I am not separated from you." 48 years are the evening, the third stage. *Adityaganas* are in it. These 48 letters are related to *jagati chhanda* of 48 letters. The *mantra* that relieves pain in this age is: "O *Adityas* in the form of *Pranas*! Connect this third stage of mine to an age of 116 years so that I am not separated from *Adityas* in *yajna* forms."

Mahidas, who knew this thoroughly and worshipped in this manner, said, "O Pain! Why are you causing this suffering to me? I cannot die of it," and he lived upto 116 years. Such worshipper remains free from diseases and lives a long life of 116 years.

Seventeenth Section: It elucidates *atma-yajna*.

Atma-yajna: A man becomes whatever feelings or thoughts he entertains. One who laughs, eats and indulges in sex reaches the source, origins or extremes of these activities. Great Rishi Angiras gave this great *mantra* to Devki's son Krishna, which is the best to recite at the time of death. "You are space. You are indestructible. You are subtle *Pran*." On hearing there words of the *Acharya*, Krishna distanced himself from other forms of worship.

Eighteenth Section: Significance of *Brahma* is described in this section. One should worship one's *mana* and the sky in the form of God. Both of them are spiritual and deity-related worships respectively. The four feet of *Brahma* are voice, smell, eyes and ears. This is spirituality. From the deity point of view the sky is *Brahma*, and its four feet are fire, air, *Aditya* and directions. These are both spiritual and deity-related preachings. Voice is the fourth leg of *Brahma*, which is lit and moved by the light of fire. *Pran* itself is the fourth leg of *manomaya Brahma*. Ears and eyes are the fourth-leg. The first three (of these four) legs are lighted by air in the form of Light, Aditya and directions. Thus a worshipper attains fame and glory and the glow of *Brahma* through this worship.

Nineteenth Section: (Worship of *Brahma* in *Aditya* form). He is Aditya. He, omniscient God, was asat (non-existent) initially. Then became *sat* (existent). Then later on unifying and concentration assumed the form of an egg. When the egg cracked open, then His organs showed themselves as silver and gold. Then the earth was formed from silver, *Dyau* (the region of light) from gold, mountains from His solid parts, clouds and fog from the subtle element, rivers from His arteries and the ocean from the water of His (urine) bladder. *Aditya* is the embryo of egg. He is *Brahma*. One who worships Him with these thoughts and feelings attains noble forms of happiness.

Fourth Chapter: It has seventeen sections.

First to Third Section: In these sections is a description of the discussion between King Janashruti and chariot riding Rajarshi Raikva.

Janashruti was a great king, known for his charity. He fed well all the people who passed from there. Once two swans were flying over his palace. One swan said, "The palace of king Janashruti is lit up with the glow of *Brahma*. Don't touch it, you will burn yourself." The other swam said, "Is it like the chariot riding king Raikva? Just as a form of dice (*krit*) in gambling wins over all other forms of dice, in the same all the piety of the subjects flows to King Raikva. Nobody knows what Raikva knows."

Janashruti also heard this. He sent people out to find out chariot riding Raikva. Then he reached him with lots of presents and requested him to enlighten about the knowledge of *Brahma*. Raikva refused. Then the king again reached there along with his daughter and repeated his request. Then Raikva, assuming the royal daughter as a means of acquiring knowledge, accepted his request.

Raikva said, "O king! One should worship *Brahma* in the form of air because everything merges into it. When the fire dies down, it merges into the air. Likewise, on drying up, water, too, merges in it. Air is present in man's body in the form of *pran*. When the body sleeps then this air in the form of *pran* merges into his senses. Air encompasses everything in itself. This is the spiritual form: *Brahma.*"

Fourth to Tenth Section: These sections deal with the story of Satyakam, the son of Jabala.

Satyakam asked his mother Jabala, "I want to go to *Gurukul,* so please tell me my *gotra* and the name of my father."

His mother said, "Sonny! Before your birth I served the guests. Then you were born. Therefore, I cannot tell you your *gotra.* You tell the *Acharya* that your name is Satyakam Jabala."

He reached Gautami Rishi and said, "*Acharya!* I want to stay with you for my *Brahmacharya Ashram* (life of celibacy as a student)."

When the *Rishi* asked for more details, he repeated the sentence of his mother. The *Rishi* felt happy and observed that *Brahma* alone could speak the truth. The *Rishi,* then performing a ceremony, entrusted him with 400 poor and weak cows for grazing, and asked him to return when the cows multiplied and grew to a thousand. Satyakam went to forest with cows, and living there started serving and tending the cows.

When the cows became a thousand, one bull said to him, "O Satyakam! The number of cows has grown to a thousand. Therefore, go to *Acharya.*"

On the way, telling him one part of secret about *Brahma,* the bull told him, "East, West, North and South—these four directions are four bright arts of *Brahma.* An aspirant who knows this brilliant piece about *Brahma* becomes famous in the world and after his death he goes to the regions of light. The other (second) aspect of this rare art will be told to you by fire god."

Further, in the way, he lit up a fire. Fire told Satyakam the second aspect of *Brahma.* The second aspect is that *Brahma* is endless. The earth, space, heaven and the ocean—these are his four arts. Knower of this truth leads a happy life on the earth, and after death reaches indestructible world. *Agni* said that the next aspect would be conveyed to you by swan, *Hans.* Next day he left with cows. In the evening when he sat with his face towards the west, a swan came flying to him and said, "The artistic actions of fire, the moon, the sun and electricity are the illuminated aspects of *Brahma.* One who knows this clearly and worships them lives a bright life in the world, and after death goes to regions of light."

The swan further said that the next aspect will be told to

him by a water fowl, named Madugu. Next day, he carried on with his journey. In the evening when he sat with his face towards the east, then the Madugu bird came and said to him: "This aspect of *Brahma* is volume or square, and is represented by pran, eyes, ears, and *mana* (heart). One who worships this aspect in his life reaches this *lok* of *Brahma* after death."

No sooner did Satyakam Jabal reach Rishi Gautam, he, on seeing him, said, "Dear! You look like one who knows *Brahma* well. Who gave you this knowledge about *Brahma*?"

Satyakam said, "I have been preached by living beings other than men. You should also kindly teach me, as I have heard that the teaching of the *guru* is the best." Then the *Acharya* taught him all the 16 arts comprehensively.

Tenth to Seventeenth Section: These sections describe the knowledge of *Brahma* imparted to Upkaushal, the disciple of Satyakam Jabala.

Upkaushal, the son of Kamal, was a *Brahmachari* of the *Ashram*. Though he had served fire for twelve years, his convocation ceremony was pending, whereas other *brahmacharis* had received their exhortation. Then Satyakam's wife, Jaya said, "Upkaushal has served fire properly. Kindly initiate him (into learning)." But Satyakam, without uttering a word, left that place. Being sad, Upkaushal resorted to hunger strike. When the *guru's* wife persuaded him to take food, he said, "There are many desires which make a man sad, I am sad, and therefore, I will not take food."

Then the fires of *yajna* talked among themselves, "He has served us well. Therefore, we should impart him the knowledge of *Brahma*." After consultation among themselves, fires said, "*Pran* is '*k*' and '*kha*' is *Brahma*."

Upkaushal said, "*Pran* I know, but what is this '*k*' and '*kha*'?" Fires replied, " '*k*' (happiness), and '*kha*' (sky)—actually both are one and the same."

In this way, Upkaushal got this teaching. Now the Family-Fire taught, "Earth, Fire, Water and Foodgrains—all these four are my forms only. The visible *Purush* in the Sun is none other than my self. A worshipper, who knows this and worships me, is free from sins."

Now the *Dakshinagni* (Southern Fire) taught, "Water, directions, stars and the moon. These are my bodies. I am the *Purush* who appears like lightning."

Now the *Avahniya Agni* (Invoking Fire) said, "*Pran*, sky, heaven and lightning—these are my four bodies. I am the *Purush* appearing in the moon."

The fires said, "Upkaushal, this knowledge, discipline or learning is *atma-vidya* or *agni-vidya*."

When the *Acharya* returned and looked at him, he observed, "You look like having attained the knowledge of *Brahma*?" Upkaushal told him all the truth. Then the *Acharya* said, "Now I will impart you that knowledge which enables man to live free and clean like lotus amidst filth of human sins."

He said, "The *Purush* visible in the eyes is fearless, indestructible *Brahma*. When ghee or water is poured into the eyes, he comes over the eyelids. He gets all the beautiful things and fruits of piety. He is in the form of light and shines like *Aditya* (the Sun) in the worlds. His worshipper has beauty and a unique glow.

"Daily activities are an expedition and the blowing wind is a certain *yajna*. It purifies the dynamic world. Voice and heart perform this *yajna*. The *yajman* (owner) of *yajna* and all the *ritwijs* (priests who help perform *yajna*) can be protected only when the *Brahma* of *yajna* is full of wisdom and knowledge and is of the best order."

Fifth Chapter

Five fires, knowledge, highest stature of *pran*, destiny of living beings, dialogue between the ancient stables and the owners of horses, and between Shvetketu and Pravahan find a mention in this chapter. It has 24 sections.

First section: It states and describes that *pran* is the best among all things.

Best Form of Pran: In body *pran* is the best and the highest. Once different senses described and called themselves the best of all. They went to Brahmaji for decision. He said, "That one is the best whose exit leaves body lifeless."

Then voice was the first to leave the body. But body continued to work like a dumb person. After that eyes, ears, heart left body one after the other. But body did not become lifeless with their departure. Now it was the turu of *pran* to leave the body. When *pran* began to leave the body, then all the senses like voice, eyes, ears etc. began to grow lax and listless. Each one was scared because body looked like becoming lifeless. They requested *pran*, "Pray don't leave the body. We have realised that you are the best of all." Therefore, the *pran* element is the best thing in the body.

Second section: It describes a *yajna-anushthan* named 'mantha'. Once the superiority of *pran* had been established, it asked, "what are my food, clothes etc?" Then senses said, "Food grains are your food and water is your clothes, because *pran* is called *anna* (Food grains) also, and water is called clothes also."

One who performs 'mantha' *anushthan* attains high status, fame and success in life. A person aspiring for these things should perform this *anushthan*. Following is the procedure of doing it:

Invocation should be sought on *amavasya* (moonless night), then on the night of *purnima* (full moon) one should prepare the *havan samagri* (ingredients for *havan yajna*) and in this curd and honey should be mixed and churned to make 'mantha' and then the remaining ghee should be mixed in *mantha* and 'ahuti' or offerings of it should be given in *havan* chanting 'Jyeshtaya shreshtaya svaha." Next *ahuti* should be 'Vasishthaya svaha'. After that

'Pratishthayaih svaha'
'Sampade svaha'
'Ayatanaya svaha'.

Offering *ahutis* with *mantras* pour ghee. Then putting both palms together as *anjali* recite the *mantra*: 'You are *pran*. You are the eldest, highest. You are the best. You are Light and Sustainer and Nurturer of all. Endow me with seniority, quality of enlightenment and nurturing. May I become everything!" Then speaking out every part of the *mantra*, eat 'mantha'. 'Tatsaviturvranimahe', 'Vayam devasya bhojanam', 'Shreshtha sarvadhatamam', 'Turam bhagasya dhimaghi',—speaking this out one should drink the wash (water) of *katori* (bowl) and spoon. Now spread the deer skin towards the west of *yajna vedi* and sleep thereon, or sleep on the ground. Have a control on your words. If you see a woman in dream, take it that you have become successful.

Third to tenth section: In these sections are described *devyan* and *pitriyan* along with knowledge related to five fires.

Once Shvetketu, the son of Aruni, went to Jeeval, the king of Panchal. Jeeval's son Pravahan asked in the royal court,

"Have you taken instructions (education) from your father?" On Shvetketu's saying 'yes', Pravahan said, "O.k. You answer these questions of mine:

1. 'Where do people go after death, after leaving this world?'
2. 'How do people return and come back?'
3. 'What is the area where *devyan* and *pitrayan* separate?'
4. 'Why is *pitralok* never filled up?'
5. 'How does this *purush* (*Brahma*) receive the fifth *ahuti* of *Soma* and ghee offered in *yajna*?'

Shvetketu could not answer these questions. On this Pravahan said, "How can that person be called educated who cannot answer these questions?"

Shvetketu came back to his father and told him all that and happened. Then Aruni said, "I myself do not know the answers to these questions". Then both father and son appeared in the royal court and expressed their desire to know answers to those questions. The king arranged for their dignified stay and in due course of tune began to explain things to them.

"The knowledge you are asking about is not available with the Brahmins. The Kshatriyas have been its preachers all over." Saying this, the king started saying.

"Heaven itself is fire. Aditya is *samidha* (wood used in *havan*) and its rays are the smoke. Day is flame and the moon is the cinders and stars are its sparks. When *shraddha* (faith) is offered in *havan*, their gods produce *Soma*.

Well known fire is *parjanya* (born for doing, working for others). The wind, clouds, lightning, to *vajra* (heavy stone), hailstorm etc.) and thunder are *samidha*, smoke, flame, cinders and sparks respectively. When the gods perform *Soma-havan* rains take place.

The earth is fire, year is *samidha*, sky the smoke, night the flame, directions are cinders and the fields are the sparks. When the gods perform the havan of rains in them, then foodgrains are produced.

Purush (man) is fire his voice is samidha, pran is smoke, tongue is the flame, eyes are cinders and ears are sparks. When the gods perform the *havan* of food grains in them, then semen is produced.

Woman is like fire. Penis is her *samidha*, *upmantran* (intercourse) is smoke, and vagina is fire. Entry is cinders and ecstasy is sparks. When the gods perform the *havan* of fire (uterus) through semen then *garbha* (conception) takes place.

In the fifth *ahuti* water becomes masculine (gender). For nine or ten months (child) remains in his mother's womb, wrapped in the umbilical cord. After being born and completing his age, he dies again, and is consigned to fire, which was the source of its origin.

When men become foresters (in *Sanyas ashram*), they are entrusted to fire. From here (i.e. from fire) they (men) in unbodied form (i.e. in soul form) are taken to *Brahmalok*. This is *devayan* way. Those who have performed their desired, satisfied (and charity-oriented) *anushthan* (deeds) reach the region of smoke. Then in an ascending order, they reach night, *Krishna paksha* (dark night), *dakshinayan* (southward), *pitralok* (the region of forefathers), sky and the moon (from one to another). The *Somarup raja* (king in *Soma* form) visible in space is the food that gods eat. They stay here till the results of their actions come to an end, and then they return through this way alone.

Now they, after transformation in smoke, change into clouds, and then rain and fall as rainfall. Then these living beings, returning as rains, become foodgrains in the form of rice. This is the most painful form of being. When people eat foodgrains then from their semen children are born, and a living being is formed in conformity with his actions. One who has done noble deeds is born as a Brahmin, the rest or others are born in three different *varnas*, ie kshatriya, vaishya, shudra. Persons indulging in sinful activities are born' as dogs and pigs, the lower forms of beings. Those who do not belong to either of the categories (i.e. men of piety or sinners) are just born and die. This is their fate.

That is why the *parlok* (the other world) is never filled up with living beings. The state of the world is contemptuous.

Thieves, drunkards, students having affairs with their teacher's wives, killers and murderers are all sinners, fallen and condemned. One who knows fully well this area of knowledge – *panchagni vidya* – is freed from bad and sinful company. He reaches pious and benevolent regions.

Eleventh to Twenty-fourth Section

Five great (categories of) men – *Prachinshal, Satya-yajna, Indradyumna, Jana* and *Budil* – have thought about what soul and *Brahma* are. When they could not arrive at any conclusion, then they reached Maharshi Udyalak, who was a great scholar, and was conversant with *Vaishvanar Vidya* dealing with the subtleties and intricacies of the soul. Maharshi Udyalak thought that he would not be able to communicate this knowledge well to these great men. Therefore, they reached King Ashvapati who was famous for his knowledge in such matters. Ashvapati welcomed all. The next day in the morning the king said to them, "I perform a *yajna*. I will pay you each as much of money as I pay to each *ritvij*. Kindly stay here with me."

All of them expressed the purpose of their coming there. The king asked them to come next morning so that he could explain to them *Vaishvanar* in the form of soul. The king asked only one question to all of them, separately – which god do you worship?

Satyayajna spoke first, "I worship Aditya."

Ashvapati said, "He (Aditya) is Vaishvanar Himself in a cosmic form. Whatever you have, either in your body or in the form of properties, are due to Him. The family of such a worshipper is bright with the glow of *Brahma*. But Aditya is only eyes, he is not total knowledge."

After this *Indradyaumna* said, "I worship air."

The king said, "Air, too, is Vaishvanar. He is the soul. All the activities of you body and all of your properties are due to Him. His worshipper is endowed with the glow of *Brahma*. But the soul is only pran. Air is not complete knowledge."

After that *Jana* said, "I worship the sky."

The king said, "He too is *Vaishvanar*. But *Vaishvanar* has only stomach; he is not complete, knowledge."

After that Budil said, "I worship water."

The king replied, "He too, certainly is Vaishvanar. But the base of the water element of body is bladder. Therefore, this water is bladder. It is not whole, complete."

Now Udyalak said, "I worship the earth."

The king said, "The earth, too, is certainly Vaishvanar in step form. She is the step of the soul in step form."

In this way *Ashvapati* satisfied the curiosity of all. In the end he said, "All of you treat *Vaishvanar atma* separately and eat it (as food). If worship is done with a feeling 'I alone am (in all things)', the feeling that he (Vaishvanar) is the soul of all, then Vaishvanar eats (food) in all *loks*, beings and souls. The forehead, eyes, *pran*, stomach bladder and both legs of this

Vaishvanar are heaven, the sun, air, sky, water and the earth respectively. He should be worshipped with this spirit. His chest, cells, heart, *mana* (mind) and face are *Vedi, darbha, garhapatya, dakshinagni*, and *avahaniya* (invoked) *agni* respectively.

This shows that all of you are the worshippers of the different parts of the self same Vaishvanar. But that Vaishvanar is inherent in every particle of this cosmos. So, how can he be worshipped in one form (part)? Vaishvanar should be worshiped with a feeling that He is inherent in all things. Air, the earth, water, sky and fire – All these five elements are found in body. This body is made of them. *Agni* is in the eyes. Water is in the bladder. Earth is legs. Air is *pran*. The sky is like forehead. This is stated to be the form of *Brahma* also. So He should be worshipped in His all-pervasive form.

Saying this, King Ashvapati instructed them about performance of *yajnas*.

Method of Performing Yajna

The first *ahuti* (offering) should be of baked food grains, and it should be rendered saying *'pranay svaha'*. It will satiate *pranas*. Then the other *ahutis* will respectively satiate eyes, *Aditya*, heaven, *Dyau* and the persons dependent on heaven. On their satiation, that Vaishvanar will be satiated with subjects, cattle, food and divine glow. The second *ahuti* should be offered saying *'vyanaj svaha'*; this will satiate *vyan*. Then with the satiation of ears, moon, directions and *Brahma* Himself, He will bestow upon the worshipper many kinds of wealth, food grains and divine glow. The third *ahuti* should be offered saying *"apanay svaha'*. It will satiate *apan*. *Apan* satiates voice, voice satiates fire, fire satiates the earth, and then from earth are satiated fire and other beings taking shelter on the earth. Fourth *ahuti* should be offered saying *'samanay svaha'*. This will satiate *saman*. This leads to satiation of *mana* (heart) and from it the *parjanya*, and from *parjanya* the electricity and from electricity the *parjanya* and others depending upon electricity. On their satiation, they acquire divine glow. The fifth *ahuti* should be given saying *'udanay svaha'*. Then skin, air, sky and others dependent upon it are satiated in the order indicated above. Then finally *bhokta* (consumer, the performer of *yajna*) is satiated.

Any *ahuti* offered without knowing this Vaishvanar is like an *ahuti* offered to ashes. But once an *agnihotra* or *yajna* is performed after comprehensive understanding of Vaishvanar, then this satiates all living beings and souls.

Sixth Chapter

Here Udyalak imparts teachings of *Brahma* to his son Shvetketu in different forms and ways. Besides, it describes the origin of creation. It has 16 sections.

First and Second Section: Origin of Creation is described in these sections. Udyalak told his son that before Creation only *Brahma* was the truth (*sat*). Then from the determination, appeared a divine glow and from it were born, water and from water the food grains.

Third and Fourth Section: Both of these sections present the *trigunatmak swarup* (nature of creation based on three attributes) of Creation. *Brahma* produced three kinds of seeds of living beings on the earth, which are *andaj*, *svedaj* and *udbhij* (ie born from egg, sweat and womb). Making clear names and forms, Brahma created 3 different forms of each seed. Brilliance of fire is in its red colour. The colour of water is white or a slight yellow; and the third black or quiet form is that of foodgrains. Fire is one but all its three forms are true. The moon and electricity, too, have three shades equally. It is because of them that the moon acquires its property of moonliness, and electricity its property of being electrical. Otherwise these words are just an indulgence of voice. Three forms are true.

Fifth Section: Here the position regarding foodgrains, water and glow is clarified. The eaten food (grains) is divided in this manner. Its solid portion turns into faeces. Its medium part transforms into flesh, and it's subtle part become *mana*. Likewise with water. Of the water, which has been drunk, the solid portion converts into urine, the medium part goes to blood, and the subtle part makes *pran*. From the solid part of *tej* (ghee, oil) are formed bones, from medium the narrow and muscles and from subtle part voice is formed

Sixth Section: Here Udyalak said that the gentle churning of curd throws up butter. Likewise the subtle part of food makes *mana*. The subtle part of water makes *pran* and the subtle part of ghee or oil produces voice.

Seventh Section: Here the position in resect of *mana* and food has been clarified.

Udyalak said, "Don't take food for fifteen days. Drink only water. Then only *pran* would be left in body, because *pran* is in water form."

Accepting the statement of his father, the son did not take food for fifteen days. He drank only water when on the 16th day he came to his father, he (father) asked him to recite *vedic mantras*. Shvetketu said, "I have forgotten them." His father said, "Just as a small spark of fire cannot burn anything, likewise out of your 16 arts (trucks, *kalas*) only one is left with you. Now go home. First take food and then come."

After meals, Shvetketu read out the *mantras*. They returned to his memory. Then Udyalak said, "Just as a small straw is capable of being burnt once a spark is given to it, likewise your one *kala* (*pran*) was inflamed by food. Therefore, *mana* is alive with food, and *pran* with water. In the same way voice also becomes knowledgeable when (it is) endowed with the glow of knowledge."

Eighth Section: The deeper meaning of life and death is explained here.

When a person sleeps, then his *jeeva* transforms into *Brahma* form, and he regains his true form. Just as an eagle, tied to a string, returns to the place of its bondage after flying around, in the same way *mana*, after wandering at various places, returns to its bondage – *pran*. The food that we eat reaches different parts of body with the help of water. All bodily activities are born of and carried through water. Therefore, one should assume (realise) that food related activities are due to *tej* (the divine in us), and *tej* is the root of *sat*. The roots of *pran* (living being) are in *sat*. This is the truth, this is my strength and glory. *Tej* reaches water (to different parts of body); *tej* is the carrier of water. The roots of water-born body are in *tej*, and the root of *tej* are in *sat*. Food, water and *tej* are transformed into different things in the body. The voice of the dead person mergers in *mana*, *mana* merges into *pran*, *pran* into *tej*, and *tej* mergers into other gods. All the energies, senses soul etc. – all things are in atomic form.

Ninth to Thirteenth Section: The situations in respect of pervasiveness of *Brahma* in all things such as honey, river, oak seed, tree and salt is described in these sections. It is said that the honeybees suck the juice from flowers, collect it in honeycombs and turn it into honey. But nobody can tell it for certain as to from which flowers specifically the juice has been picked up and collected. Likewise the knower of *Brahma* does not know as to from which source his inspiration came. One who knows *Brahma* transforms himself into and becomes *Brahma* himself. Then he does not find any difference between himself and *Brahma.*

Likewise, the rivers may flow anywhere. But once they submerge themselves into ocean, they become ocean. Then nobody can distinguish in water as to which river it belongs. The same is the case of the knower of Brahma.

If you hurt or harm the roots or trunk of a tree, some juice will flow out of it. That juice, or *rasa,* is *Brahma* himself, his (tree's) *jeevatma.* If this *rasa* or its *jeeva* form dries up, the tree, too, will dry up. It will die of drying up. But its *rasa,* the *jeeva* form, does not die. Likewise, there are seeds in flowers. You can see them, but you cannot see the huge tree hidden in the seed. That is the subtle truth – *Brahma.*

Udyalak asked his son to bring a little salt, and get it placed in water. Salt dissolved in water. The father said, "Take the salt out of it." The son could not take it out because *Brahma* had dissolved. The father asked his son to drink that glass of water, at the top, in the middle and bottom. After drinking the son observed that the water was salty all through. His father said that just as he could not see the salt spread over to all (sides of) water, in the same way *Brahma* was all-pervasive, but no one could see Him. But one who knows Him, is a *Brahma-gyani,* can see and realise Him everywhere.

Fourteenth to Sixteenth Section: The subtle form of soul is described in these sections. One who does not recognize the very existence of God suffers from the biggest obstacle in his path of being a *Brahma-gyani.* He does not know what soul, what God is. *Brahma* is in the nature of truth. In a subtle form He pervades every atom. As long as *pran* is in human body, he recognizes all, speaks and performs all activities; but once the subtle *pran* leaves the body it becomes inactive, dead i.e. the body becomes lifeless.

So, the subtle element, *Brahma,* pervades all over. One who has realised this fact becomes *Brahma-gyani, Brahma* himself.

Seventh Chapter

It has 26 sections, clarifying *Brahma* from different angles.

First to Fifteenth Section: *Brahma* has been explained and clarified through various names, forms etc. Once Devarshi Narad said to Sanat Kumar, 'Lord! Instruct me regarding *Brahma*.' Sanat Kumar asked, 'What is the limit of your knowledge?' Narad replied, "I know a little bit about *Rag-Veda*, other *Vedas*, history and *Puranas*. But I am totally ignorant about soul."

Sanat Kumar said, "Whatever you know about the *Vedas* all that is just names. Worship names. One who worships *Brahma* in name form will meet his desired end."

Devarshi Narad expressed his desire to know more and go beyond names, then Sanat Kumar said, "Voice is above names, because it experiences these various things, *Sankalpa* or determination is above *mana*, because it inspires. *Chittha* or consciousness is above *sankalpa*, because everything merges into it and is lodged there. Contemplation is superior to *Chittha*, because it is the strength of contemplation which endows significance to all things in the world. *Vigyan*, special or specific knowledge, or science is above contemplation because all things are realised through special knowledge. Strength far exceeds science because it is through strength that science is won, conquered. *Anna* or food grains are superior to strength, because this alone makes a man strong. Water is above *anna*, because it is the favour or otherwise of water which makes one happy or sad. *Tej* (glow, brilliance, lit up heat) is superior to water, because it is the heat of *tej* that creates water. Sky is superior to *tej* because the sun and the moon are located there and it is because of it that human beings speak, hear, grow and are born. Memory (*Smar, Smaran*) is above, superior to the sky, because this alone leads one to knowledge or ignorance. Hope is bigger than memory because the hope inspired memory forces one to do things including the reading and recital of *mantras*. *Pran* is above hope, because the whole world is located in the, is inhered in it. Because this is *Brahma*, *Brahma* is the fixed and moving, entire world; He pervades everywhere. *Pran* is *Brahma*, and *Brahma* is *pran*."

Sixteenth to Twenty Second Section: Pervasiveness of truth, faith and action have been described in these sections.

It is stated that the search for truth is done is a special manner i.e. through contemplation. You need faith for contemplation. Faith alone makes contemplation possible, and one who is committed is the one who is faithful.

Action leads to commitment. Therefore, the object of search is basically action. Creation (action) is possible only after attaining happiness. If one is unhappy, he cannot create.

Therefore, happiness is basically and specifically the object of knowing.

Twenty-Third to Twenty-Sixth Section: *Sukh* or happiness is *bhuma*. *Bhuma* means extensive, unbounded, limitless, *Virat Purush* (ie God), glory etc. This *bhuma* is *Brahma* Himself; it is pervasive all over. This is the soul, God. One who realises it becomes *Brahma* Himself.

Eighth Chapter

This chapter, having fifteen sections, deals with the position of soul located in body.

First to Fifteenth Section: In these sections the position of soul in the body and the nature of soul have been described. God has been explained in *saguna* form, i.e. having appearance.

Like the earth, the sky and heaven visible outside in the physical world, the earth, the sky and the heaven are located in heart also. They have fire, air and the sun etc. i.e. all. Though they are so big, vast and extensive, they exist in subtle form. Slowly and slowly this body becomes weak; from birth to the old age the body goes on becoming weaker and weaker and finally meets its death one day i.e. the subtle soul, which is in nature *Brahma* Himself leaves this body and it is called the death of the body. That is why this body is called mortal. But the soul (*Brahma*) located in the body neither grows old nor dies. It is this knowledge which man does not try to get; and in his ignorance he keeps himself ensnared and wandering in the cobweb of the worldly *maya* or illusions. But one who attains this knowledge becomes wise and transforms himself into *Brahma* itself.

Once Indra and demon king Virochan went to Brahmaji to know the truth about soul (*Brahma*) and stayed there and lived a life of celibacy and austere discipline for thirty-two years. Then Prajapati asked them the purpose of their visit. On knowing their objective, Brahmaji said that the *Purush* you see in the eyes is the fearless and nectar-like *Brahma*. Both of them saw the reflection growing in the eyes and thought it to be soul. Then they saw the reflection in water and mirror asked, who was that. Prajapati replied, "The self-same *Brahma* is in their reflection, too."

On knowing and understanding this, both of them went back to their respective regions. Virochan preached to all others that the soul was Brahma and they should worship it. On the other hand, Indra pondered that body was mortal. Will the soul, too, die with the death of body? He stayed with Brahmaji for another thirty-two years leading a life of discipline and celibacy in order to remove his doubts in this regard.

Then Brahmaji told him, "The *Purush* you see in dreams is *Brahma*, the soul." Indra came back but he was not satisfied. Finally, he went back to Brahmaji and stayed there for yet another thirty-two years with celibacy.

Then Brahmaji said, "In the state of sleep when there is peace, and no dreams, then the soul in body is the fearless, immortal *Brahma*." Even then the curiosity of Indra was not satisfied. He thought, "In this state (of sleep) the soul does not know itself or other objects. Then how does it know who it is and from where has it come?" Indra again approached Brahmaji with his curiosity.

Brahmiaji said, "Fine. You stay with me for another fifty years and lead a life of perfect discipline." Indra stayed there for fifty years. Thus he stayed there in all for 101 years living a life of celibacy and austere discipline. Then Brahmaji told him: "Body is mortal. It is surrounded with death. But the immortal bodiless soul lives in this body. Though staying with and in this body, it is free from the feelings of joy, pain, likes and dislikes etc. Just as the wind, lightning, clouds and their thunder are bodiless, and as they assume forms, lit up by the best light of the sun, in the same way the body too as if flying gets its real form on attaining the supreme light of *Brahma*. He is the noblest *Purush*. One who knows this secret, the mysterious knowledge, is the wise person and is the knowledgeable. He knows *Brahma* and merges himself in Him. We are that person (*Purush*, God)."

(3) *Vajrasuchik Upnishad*

The word 'Brahmin' has been clarified in this *Upnishad*. There are four *varnas* – *Brahmin*, *kshatriya*, *vaishya* and *shudra* – according to the Vedas and *Smritis*. Chief among them is

'*Brahmin*'. The question is: 'What is a *Brahmin?*'

Jeeva is only one who according to his actions assumes different bodies. Body cannot be *Brahma*. All human bodies have the five elements, leading to old age, decay and mortality. This, too, is uncertain that a *Brahmin* will invariably be fair, or a *kshatriya* be of red complexion, or for that matter the *vaishya* be of yellow colour and a *shudra* black.

When a person burns or cremates the dead body of his father, he is not changed with the sin of *Brahma-hatya* (ie killing a *Brahmin*). So body is not *Brahmin*. Many *Rishis* were born in different castes. For example Shrangi Rishi was born of *Mrigi* or Kaushik was born of *Kusha*. So one is not a *Brahmin* by caste. Knowledge, too, is not Brahmin because many highly wise and knowledgeable persons were born in the *kshatriya* caste. *Jeeva* performs actions. Therefore, actions, too, are not Brahmin. Religiosity, too, is not Brahmin because many *kshatriyas*, too, have given away gold in charity. Then religion, too, is not Brahmin.

So, who, finally is a Brahmin? The question bounces back.

A Brahmin is one who has the feeling of non-dualism; one who is devoid of caste, attributes and actions, one who is free from the defects of 6 *urmies* (urges, instincts) and 6 feelings; one who is endowed with true knowledge and happiness; one who is free from affections and desires, one who knows the supreme truth and has completely renounced his ego. That man alone is entitled to be called a Brahmin. One should acknowledge and accept that man only as Brahmin who experiences the qualities of being *sachchidanand* – truth, consciousness and joy, and none else. In brief, in essence, these are the characteristics of a Brahmin.

(4) *Jabal Darshan Upnishad*

This Upnishad has ten sections, dealing in detail with the *yoga* element –

First section: It describes different parts of *yoga*. Yoga philosophy has eight parts. They are : *Yam, Niyam* (rules), *Asan* (postures), *Pranayam, Pratyahar, Dhyan* (contemplation), *Dharana*, and *Samadhi* (trance). *Yam* has ten different parts, namely, *satya* (truth), *ahinsa* (non-violence), *astiya* (non-stealing), *Daya* (kindness), *arjav Brahmacharya* (celibacy), *Kshama* (forgiveness), *dhriti* (patience), *mitahar* (eating less) and *shuchita* (purity of mind). *Yoga* can yield good results by adherence to these rules and regulations, and not otherwise.

Second Section: This section describes rules. There are ten, namely *tapa* (hard work), *santosh* (contentment), *lajja* (sensitiveness, sense of shame), *Ishwar-puja* (worship of God), *astikata* (faith), *dan* (charity), *vrat* (fasting), *japa* (recital of God's name), mati (good sense), and listening to good principles.

Third Section: It describes various *asanas*. There are nine kinds of *asanas*: *Swastik, Gomukh, Padmasan, Veerasan, Bhadrasan, Muktasan, Singhasan, Mayurasan* and *Sukhasan*.

Fourth Section: It describes nerves and self-knowledge.

Human body is equal to 96 *anguls* (finger-width). In its centre the place is occupied by fire. The middle portion of the body is two *anguls* above thigh joints and two *anguls* below penis. This is *muladhar* (base). Nine *anguls* above is *kand*. In the centre of *kand* is *nabhi* (navel). The nerve fo the central part of *kand* is *sushumna*. There are seventy-two thousand nerves on all its four sides. Among them the prominent nerves are – *sushumna, pingla, ira, saraswati, pusha, varuna, hastajivha, yashasvini, alambusa, kuhu, vishvodara, tapasvini, shankhini,* and *gandhari*. Three among them are more important and *sushumna* is the chief among them. It is called *Brahma-nadi* also.

Human body is just a bundle of nerves. Always take it as one of no consequence. However, the man who knows, like the indestructible God residing in him, that he too is God and lives patiently is rid of all sorrows. When a man is capable of destroying the ignorance making distinction between man and God and realises the God in himself, he becomes *Brahma-gyani*.

Fifth Section: It deals with the processing or purification of nerves and self.

Nadi–shodhan or purification of nerves: For this one should observe the rules prescribed and practise according to the instructions of *shastras* (classics). One should give up desires and determinations. Sit in a lonely and clean place. Keep your head neck and body erect, and sit quiet. Imagine a big halo of moon on the tip of your nose. Contemplate a *pranav (Om)* point there, and further imagine that a nectar-like substance is flowing from *Brahma* in a *turiya* form (quiet, etherialised). Draw air in through *ira* nerve in your stomach, and contemplate about fire located in the centre of your body. Then imagine that flames are rising up in the air you have drawn in (inhaled) – experience it. Then contemplate of a fire seed, tree from point and sound, and then throw air out (exhale) through *pingla.*

Practise this daily for three or four days. Or do this thrice daily during your moon and evening prayers. One set of breathing may consist of inhaling and exhaling six times. This purifies nerves.

Atma-shodhan: Soul is pure and self-lit. It is dirty due to ignorance and acquisition of knowledge purifies it. When the filth of ignorance is washed with the water of knowledge a man becomes totally purified and clean. But a man enmeshed in worldly affairs finds it difficult to cleanse himself.

Sixth section describes various processes of doing *pranayam* and the good results emanating from it.

Seventh Section: *Pratyahar* is explained here in a number of ways. *Pratyahar* means that a man submits and surrenders to *Brahma* all the good and bad deeds, thoughts and things which he has been doing all through his life. Performing one's daily deeds and indulging in desires in the course of worship of *Brahma* is *pratyahar.* Concentrate and give up self-consciousness and self-wisdom, and place your mind in quiet, desireless soul. Those who have realised *Brahma* face to face have described this practice as *pratyahar.*

Eighth Section: *Dharana* is explained here. It is stated that there are five kinds of *dharanas.* They are to contemplate the outside sky in the sky located in body, the outside air in *pran,* the outside fire in the fire of the belly, the outside water in the water inside body and to contemplate the whole earth in the physical parts of body.

Ninth Section: Contemplation has been described in this section. Two varieties of contemplation have been mentioned. In one, one assumes 'Soaham' about God. In the second, one contemplates with the assumption, 'I am *Brahma* myself.'

Samadhi has been described in the tenth section. Decisive knowledge that *Paramatma* (God) and *Jeevatma* are one is called *samadhi.*

(5) *Jabalya Upnishad*

This *Upnishad* describes the questions and answers between

Lord Jabali and Pippaladi. It is related to *Shaivite* philosophy.

Lord Jabali told Pippaladi that when Pashupati Shiva, imbued with ego, assumes the form of worldly *jeeva* or *pran*, then he is called *Pashu* or animal. Five elements are *pashupati*. A living being or *jeeva* is *pashu* because of his birth in this world. The owner or lord of the living beings is *Ishwar*, ie God, and therefore He is *Pashupati* (*Shiva*).

Pappaladi asked, 'How is knowledge attained?'

Jabali replied: 'By applying *vibhuti* or ashes. Put it on forehead in three horizontal lines and apply it to chest and shoulders also. All the experts of the *Vedas* have called it *Shambhav vrat* in different *Vedas*. One attains salvation by applying or wearing this *vibhuti* in *tripund* (three lines) form is related to the Shaiviti philosophy and its followers.

(6) *Maitreya Upnishad*

It has three chapters.

First Chapter: It describes the dialogue between Brihadratha and Shakayanya Muni.

Shakayanya Muni tells the king if one can apply one's mind to *Brahma* with the same intensity and involvement, with which it is involved in worldly pursuits, one can attain salvation. The soul residing in one's heart is witness to all actions. One cannot know God through mind or voice. He is in all things, including the beginning and the end. He is Himself self-lit, rare, fixed and steadfast, strange, serious, lonely and in the nature of emancipation. He is the highest bliss; He has assumed all forms of beings directly and this soul itself is *Paramatma*.

Second Chapter: There is a discussion between Maharshi Maitreya and Shiva in this chapter. They are talking about the supreme element. Shiva has called human body a temple. The *jeevatma* residing in it is Shiva himself. Therefore, knowing that 'I am that' one should worship *Brahma*. The real knowledge is to know the fact that there is no difference between *atma* and *Paramatma*. He Himself is *jeeva*; He Himself is *Brahma*.

Third Chapter: Here it has been clarified as to who is *Brahma*. The mystery has been unravelled by *Brahma* Himself.

I myself am *Brahma*. I am there in the entire fixed and moving world in the whole cosmos. I am in every single particle. I am *Omkar*. Duality, non-duality, *Brahma*, Vishnu, Mahesh

(Rudra) – I am all these forms of *Paramatma*. Whatever is there in this world is *Brahma* Himself. He Himself is soul as well as *Paramatma*. One who has this knowledge has become *Brahma* Himself.

(7) *Kundik Upnishad*

This *Upnishad* deals with various activities of a *Sanyasin* when he enters into and lives in *Sanyas Ashram*.

When a disciple completes his studies of the *Vedas* and his *Brahmacharya Ashram* comes to an end, and he is asked by his *guru* to go home, then this disciple is called an *Ashrami*. After entering into *Grihastha Ashram* (family life) also one should continue to perform the worship and *yajna* of *Brahma*. After that one should give up and leave all things to his sons, and go and wander in the forest. He should make *kand-mul*, ie root fruits, vegetables and water and air his food. A *sanyasin* should give up everything except *Kamandal* (a vessel for water), tongs, doublet, loin-cloth and *dhoti* etc. A *sanyasin* should think about himself. "I am unimaginable like the sky. I am unlimited like the ocean. I am *Narayan, Purari* and whole and I am God and have all this attributes." In other words, he should conduct like he is perceiving *Brahma* in everything. See himself in all men and things. Become *Brahma* Himself.

(8) *Arunik Upnishad*

In this *Upnishad* Brahmaji preached the teaching of *Sanyas* to Aruni, the son of Arun.

Once Aruni reached the region of Prajapati and asked him, "Lord! How should I give up all actions?" Pajapati replied, "Son! One should give up brothers, friends, tuft of hair on head, the sacred thread, the study and performance of *yajna*. Not only this, one should renounce even the desire for all worlds such as *Bhuh, Bhuvah, Svah, Mahah* etc. One should renounce everything except *dand* (staff), loin-cloth and a doublet. Whether a *Brahmachari* (celibate) or a *Grihastha* (man of family) one should throw one's sacred thread in water and instead wear in heart the inner thread of *Brahma*. In other words, one should remember only *Brahma* and see and perceive Him in everything.

"I have accepted *Sunyas*", one should repeat this thrice to himself. Then one should take *dand* pronounicng this *mantra*,

"May all the living beings be unafraid of me." In other words, give up everything. When you go to a village or town pronounce 'Om' thrice and beg and accept alms. The *Sanyasins* who become completely desireless and worship God in the most sustained and disciplined manner reach their highest goal. Such wise and learned *sanyasins* reach the highest status and like the sun placed at the top and lighting every thing, see everything in the light of God.

(9) *Sanyas Upnishad*

This *Upnishad* deals with issues related to *Sanyas*.

A *Sanyasin* should take food to keep his body and soul together, just to live. Otherwise, he should give up everything. For a *sanyasin*, contemplation is his sacred thread, knowledge is his tuft of hair on head a water pond is his vessel, and its bank is his place of living. A *sanyasin* is one whose all the forty *sanskaras* have been performed; he is totally detached; his mind is pure and calm; he is free from desires and anger; he is rich and endowed with *dharma*, true action, real affections and is emancipated.

Some categories of persons are just incompetent to accept or go into *sanyas*; e.g. those who have fallen from the standards of *sanyas*, one who preaches to his wife, one who obstructs in accepting *sanyas*, a downfallen or a man of feminine nature, disabled, deaf, dumb, a child, a hypocrite, diplomatic, sexy, domestic servant, teacher, an atheist, or a person lacking in good manners. Such persons, even if they accept *sanyas*, should not preach to others.

In other words, the conduct of a *sanyasin* should be pure, holy and like that of an innocent child. He should give up all desires and affections and devote his heart and mind in the worship of *Brahma*. His sole aim should be to attain salvation. the *sanyasins* are of six kinds: *bahudak, kutichak, hans, paramhans, avadhoot* and *turiyateet*.

(10) *Yoga Chudamani Upnishad*

This *Upnishad* deals with attainment of self-knowledge by practising various parts of *yoga* and achieving perfection and success in their practice.

The six rules of *yoga-sadhana* are *Asan pranayam, pratyahar, dharana, dhyan* and *samadhi*. Main among the *asanas* in priority are *Siddhasan, kamalasan* and *padmasan.* A *yogi* cannot achieve perfection or *siddhi* without seeing in his own body the six *chakras*, sixteen bases (*adhar*) and five skies.

Purak, kumbhak and *rechak* – all these three are just another form of *pranav, Om* or God. An *Omkar pranayam* is one in which its practitioner repeats *purak* twelve times, *kumbhak* sixteen times and *rechak* ten times. The best *pranayam* is one performed 36 times; the medium one has 24 repetitions and the most ordinary has twelve repetitions.

It is assumed that *pranayam* is that fuel which burns away sinful actions. *Asanas* destroy diseases and *pranayam* sins. The evils of heart can be rid of through *pratyahar* only. *Dharana* brings composure to a *yogi's* mind. He becomes patient. Through *samadhi* he attains rare *Chaitanya Brahma* (God as a conscious light). Then, this (*yoga*) destroys all the good and bad actions of *yogi* and he attains salvation.

(11) *Mah Upnishad*

This *Upnishad* describes the immense form of Shri Narayan. The whole thing has been presented as a dialogue between King Janak and Shukadev. It has six chapters –

First chapter describes the form and nature of Narayan. Narayan is the God of the whole universe. He is the basis, the prime cause of this universe. The whole cosmos is inherent in Him.

Second chapter describes the world and *jeeva*. Here Shukdevji asks King Janak to teach him about the basic element, its various forms and effulgence.

King Jank replies, saying, "The whole world of fixed and moving objects is just an illusion. Once you know its illusory nature your ignorance disappears and your mind becomes pure. This knowledge leads you to peace equivalent to salvation strong attachment to worldly objects is the cause of bondage, and the end of desires for these things leads one to salvation. Only that *jeeva* is rid and free who maintains himself detached as a witness to all things (himself having no desire or affections); does not have craving for fruits and results; gives up all thinking including that of *dharma* and *adharma*; becomes indifferent to the whole labyrinth of the universe; one who sees fullness and perfection in his own soul. The pleasure that he gets in this state of mind is the realisation of *Brahma.*"

Third chapter describes things related to detachment (disaffection).

One *muni*, named Nidagh, left for pilgrimage in his childhood. He took bath at three and half crore places of religious pilgrimage and then he returned to his father, Ribhu and said, "This world is subject to decay and destruction. It seems to have been made for death itself. Its entire glories are painful. But heart, as a magnet, keeps them all together and united. *Lakshmi* (wealth) produces affections and greed. Relatives are a source of tragedy. Like the drops falling from the edge of a leaf, man's life, too is being destroyed in a moment." With ideas of this sort he has proved that the world is just an ocean of woes. He said, "Poison kills one life, but (objects of) affections kill many lives. The defects and shortcomings of my mind have been removed. Though I live amidst this mirage, I am miles and miles away from (objects of) temptations.

In the fourth chapter Ribhu imparts instructions to his son Nidagh regarding *Brahma* through four doors of salvation. "My son! You know everything. Nothing is secret to you, now. There are four doors leading to salvation: *Sham* (restraint), *Vichar* (thinking and contemplation), *Santosh* (contentment) and *Satsang* (good company). You adopt and master any one of them. The rest three would be automatically controlled. First of all a man should sharpen (and increase) one's intelligence through the study of classics and the company of the wise persons. Then alone one attains salvation. An eye enthralled with touch, words etc. is useless. All this visible labyrinth is just one form of *Pranav* (God). This visible universe is just part of *THAT CHITTA* (*Chaitanya Brahma*). Therefore, try to attain Him only; because then alone you will get salvation.

In the fifth chapter Ribhu elaborates to his son Nidagh the seven backgrounds of knowledge and ignorance.

Backgrounds of knowledge: *Shubhechchha* (good intentions) *vicharana* (contemplation), *Tanumanasi, asansakti* (detachment), *padartha bhavana* (love for objects) and *turyaga* – these are seven backgrounds of knowledge. Once you are free from them, you are free from sufferings for ever.

Backgrounds of Ignorance: *Beej –Jagrit, jagrit, mahajagrit, jagritswapna, swapna, swapne-jagrit* and *sushupti* (sleep): These are the states of ignorance, affection. One entertains the feeling of 'yours' and 'mine' due to ignorance, only a wise person attains salvation, who becomes aware of these various states of ignorance.

Man's different thinkings, decisions and determinations are explained in the sixth chapter. Chief among them are riddance from passions, the state and plight of the ignorant persons, and the realization of *Paramatma*, God.

(12) *Rudraksha Jabal Upnishad*

This *Upnishad* describes things related to Rudraksha. The story of Rudraksha in brief is this: The fiery Rudra himself has stated that while contemplating ways of killing the demon Tripur, he closed his eyes. At that time some drops of tears fell on the ground and turned into Rudraksha. Later trees (of Rudraksha) also sprang up from these tears. A Rudrakswha equal to the size of *amla* fruit is considered the best. A smaller Rudraksha of the size of gram is the worst, and one equal to the size of a berry is considered of medium quality.

Who should wear a Rudraksha, and of what kind? A Brahmin should wear a Rudraksha of white colour; a kshatriya of red colour; a vaishya of yellow colour; and a shudra of black colour.

Benevolent Rudraksha: Rudraksha of equal size smooth, hard and thorny are good.

Malevolent Rudraksha: It has the following six defects: Moth eaten, broken, without thorns, ugly and bearing scars.

The best Rudraksha is one that has a hole by itself.

A medium Rudraksha is one in which you have to bore a hole forcibly.

How many and how a Rudraksha is to be worn? Wear a Rudraksha to worship Shiva. One should wear a sting of one Rudraksha on heart or on tuft of hair on head. If worn round the head, then the string should have 3 Rudrakshas. One should wear a string of 36 Rudrakshas around neck, or 16 numbers each on both arms, of 12 numbers each on wrists. If worm on the shoulder, it should have 15 Rudrakshas; and if one is wearing it like the sacred thread (*janeu*) then it should have 108 beads. One can wear round one's neck strings of

Rudraksha having 2, 3, 5 or seven sounds, as ear sings, or around neck as garlands. Specially tied Rudrakshas can be worn as armlets, both in sleep and while one is awake.

Wearing a thousand Rudrakshas is called the best, wearing 500 is medium, and wearing 300 is considered the worst.

Wear them like this: Chant 'Ishan' mantra when you intend to wear on head; chant 'tatya purushen' if you propose to wear round your throat / neck; and chant 'aghor' mantra if you propose to wear near your heart. Intelligent persons should wear Rudraksha on their hands accompanied to the chant of 'aghor' beej mantra. They should be charmed with the five-syllable mantra of Shiva (Om namah Shivay). Then one should prepare its strings chanting basic mantra and wear 3, 5, or 7 strings.

Eyes and effects: One-eyed Rudraksha: It is just another form of the supreme element (Brahma). By wearing it one controls one's senses and its wearer merges in the supreme element.

Two-eyed Rudraksha: This Rudraksha has the form of Ardhanarishwar (one of the forms of Shiva). Lord Ardhanarishwar is always kind and happy with the man who wears it.

Three-eyed Rudraksha: It represents all the three fires- Garhapatya (of family), Avhaniya (invocative) and Dakshinagni. Agnidev is always happy with the person who wears it.

Four-eyed Rudraksha: It represents Brahma. Its wearer always enjoys the blessings of Brahma.

Five-eyed Rudradsha: It represents five-faced Shiva. Lord Shiva is always kind to its wearer.

Six-eyed Rudraksha: It represents Lord Kartikey. Its wearer remains healthy, free from diseases, and is blessed with wealth. It is considered a representative of Ganesh also. Its wearer is blessed with good sense, purity and wealth.

Seven-eyed Rudraksha: It represents Brahmi and other mothers. Its wearer gets good health and wealth.

Eight-eyed Rudraksha: It represents 8 Bhagawatis and 8 vasus. Mother Ganges too remains happy with its wearer.

Nine-eyed Rudraksha: It represents the power of nine gods. These powers remain happy with, and bless its wearer.

Ten-eyed Rudraksha: It represents Yama, the lord of Death. You experience peace just by seeing it.

Eleven-eyed Rudraksha: Its represents 11 Rudras. These gods bestow good luck to its wearer.

Twelve-eyed Rudraksha: It represents Lord Vishnu and 12 Adityas. Those who worship them, wear it.

Thirteen-eyed Rudraksha: This is considered fortunate, and grants all wishes. Lord cupid blesses its wearer immensely.

Fourteen-eyed Rudraksha: It removes and cures all diseases. On wearing it, you should give up onion, garlic, wine, meat and other related food stuffs.

It is said that if you start wearing Rudraksha when there is eclipse, or there is *Vishuvat sankranti* or when *ayan* is changing or on a full moon night or moonless night, you are rid of all sins there and then.

It is presumed that the basic part of Rudraksha is *Brahma*, the inner hole is Vishnu and its eyes (faces) are Rudra, and all its points are imbued with all gods.

(13) *Garuda Upnishad*

Garuda vidya has been described in this *Upnishad*.

The following *mantra* should be recited with heart touching other parts of body. *Om namah* (touching thumb), *Shri Garudaya* (through the middle finger), *Shri Vishnuwallabhaya* (through *anamika*, the last but one finger), *trailokyaprapujitaya* (through the last finger) and *ugrabhayankar kalanalrupaya* (through the palm of one's hand). After that one contemplates of Shri Garuda. Eight *mantras* such as 'Swastiko dakshinam padam' etc. are recited mentally. In essence they mean that the right leg of Lord Garuda is in the shape of *swastika* and the left leg is folded in. Lord Vishnu likes him immensely. Poisonous snakes such as *Katak, Yajnasutra, Vasuki* and *Takshak* form his waistbands and garlands round his neck. He wears *padma* and *mahapadma* in his ears. Paudra and Kalika fan him. His sons are always at his service. His complexion is rather yellow, and he has the glow of gold on his face, his arms are long and shoulders broad. He wears many ornaments. Upto thighs his colour is gold, and a divine light emanates from his back. Upto his neck his colour is red like *kumkum*. His face shines with the brightness of hundreds of moons. His nose is blue in front and slightly twisted. The *kundals* in His ears are beautiful. His teeth are strong and awe-inspiring, and He wears a bright crown. The whole body displays the reddishness of *kumkum* and face a brightness. O the carrier of Vishnu! Our salutations to Thee."

One who contemplates Garuda in this fashion thrice daily is rid of all poisons. One who listens or studies this sombre secret on a moonless night is never bitten by snake.

(14) *Savitri Upnishad*

This *Upnishad* describes the status of *Savita* and *Savitri*, and their pervasive character.

Savita – Savitri: *Agni* (fire) is Savita and the earth Savitri. They are two beings, forming one pair. The air is Savita, and the sky is Savitri. Where there is air, there is sky. *Yajna* is Savita and *Chhanda* (stanza) Savitri, Savita and Savitri are related to each other and are all-pervasive.

The first step of Savitri is '*tatsaviturvarenyam*' ie Savita is worthy of being chosen, taken; the second step is '*bhargo devasya dhimahi*', ie we contemplate the glory, fame of God. The third step is '*dhiyo yo nah prachodayat*', ie it should inspire our minds, intellects. The *Rishi Virat Purush* and stanzas and gods of the *vidyas* (disciplines or studies) of *Bal* (strength) and *Atibal* (super strength) – both are Savitri. I always experience the flawless *Pranav* and the gods known as *Bal* (like the vast sun) and *Atibal*. After contemplating in this manner, one performs an *anushthan* of the *mantra* 'Om hrim bale'. This does away the feeling of hunger. He controls his appetite. The knower of this *Savitri vidya* reaches *Savitri-lok*.

Upnishads Related to Atharva Veda

The main *Upnishads* related to the *Atharva Veda* are as follows:

1. *Mandukya Upnishad*
2. *Atharvashir Upnishad*
3. *Parabrahma Upnishad*
4. *Mahavakya Upnishad*
5. *Atma Upnishad*
6. *Gopalpurvatapaniya Upnishad*
7. *Krishna Upnishad*
8. *Ganapati Upnishad*
9. *Sharabh Upnishad*
10. *Devi Upnishad*
11. *Sita Upnishad*
12. *Surya Upnishad*
13. *Prashna Upnishad*
14. *Mundak Upnishad*

Let us see what do the *Upnishads* related to this *Veda* say. The invocation of peace of there *Upnishads* is like this:

"*Om bhadram karnebhih, shrunuyam devam bhadram pashyemakshabhiryajatrah |*
Sthire rangaistushtuvam sastanribhirvyashem devahitam yadayuh | |
Svasti na Indro vridhashrawah swasti na pusha vishvavedah |
Swasti nastarkshyo arishtanemih swasti no brihaspatirdadhatu | |
Om Shantih shantih shantih."

"O God! May we hear the words of welfare with our ears; see scenes of welfare with our eyes! May we get (long) age like that of gods, with all parts of our body working well! May the sun do good things to us, may Braihaspati, who destroys all obstacles, do good to us!"

(1) *Mandukya Upnishad*

In this *Upnishad* of the *Atharvaveda* 'Om' has been explained. Its steps and stages and *matras* have been given in detail.

The letter 'Om' is *Brahma* in nature. He is the whole universe. It has four states.

First state: The state of dream is the *antahpragya* (the knowledge of which pervades the subtle world) state of *Brahma*. It has seven parts (seven *loks*, seven rays) and nineteen faces (ten senses, five pranas and four *antahkarana*).

Second state: When a man is asleep, he does not entertain any desire, and does not even see a dream. This is called the state of sleep

Third state: This state is one of unified, concentrated happiness. During this third state of special knowledge the person has limited knowledge but he is enjoying and consummating happiness.

Fourth state: In this state the person is sub-conscious both internally and externally. It is not one of narrow knowledge, and is neither visible. It is one in which there is no conduct, inaccessible, it has no attributes, is beyond thoughts and description. It is uniform, quintessential, peaceful, witnessing all the labyrinths of the world. This is the fourth state. Both the soul as well as *Param Brahma* are in the form of syllable 'Om' or 'Aum', and it has *matras*. *Matras* are the dissected parts and the dissected parts are the *matras*. This 'Aum' is formed with a combination of 'A', 'U' and 'M'.

(2) *Atharvashir Upnishad*

In this *Upnishad*, Rudra has been worshipped as God, and in contains description regarding the origin of water and the three *gunas—Raj, Sat, Tam*.

Once gods reached *Rudra lok* and asked Rudra:

"Who are you?"

Rudra said, "I am one who is everything. I am the past, the present and the future. I am everything. I am inside-outside, in all directions; I am the eternal and the daily, *Brahma* and non-*Brahma*, women, men, *Gayatri* etc. *Chhanda, Garhapatya* (family life) etc.; *Agni, Pruth,* cow, pleasant and ennobled tellings of rosary, *tej* (glow), light etc. – I am all. One who knows me, knows the *Vedas* as well.

Then the gods paid their obeisance to him and said, "O Rudra! You are Brahma, Vishnu. You are *Brahma*. *Bhuh, Bhuvah, Svah* – are respectively your lower, middle parts and head. You are in all. You are the world and show yourself in many forms. You are *Soma*. You are nectar. According to the *Vedas* water (You) is the base origin of this creation. After that egg, air *Brahma* and *Savitri, loks* etc. were born in this creation. Then in the world truth was discovered with great perseverance, and later eternity (perennial-ness) was realised through *angul pravah* (in tense and rustained devotion). Water alone is light, *rasa*, nectar, *Brahma*, *Bhuh*, *Bhuvah*, *Svah* and *namah*. This gave rise to Creation.

Then Lord Rudra said that the one-time, two-time and three-time reader / student of this *Upnishad* obtains the right to holy activities, status of Ganapati, and entry into '*Om*'.

(3) *Parabrahma Upnishad*

This *Upnishad* is a critique of the realisation of *Para-Brahma* through the practices of *Sanyas ashram*.

In this *Upnishad* Lord Pippalad tells Shaunak Rishi that before the creation only *Brahma* existed. Then with an expression of His desire, He created this world of fixed and moving objects. He pervades its every single particle. You cannot assess that *Para Brahma* truth only by listening to others; you can know and realise Him through your own experience only. Just as you feel heat only on touching and not through someone's saying likewise for obtaining knowledge of *Brahma* you have to undergo severe and serious devotion through *Yoga*. It is only then that you realise Him.

Like a *Sanyasin* committed to truth and sincerity you can obtain Him through honest and transparent conduct; but a *sanyasin*, too, has to strictly perform his duties. Man cannot become a *sanyasin* just by wearing a sacred thread on his body. He has to wear the real sacred thread of knowledge, the knowledge of *Brahma*. To know *Brahma*, one has to answer to himself: Who is He? What is His nature? A real aspirant who has striven for and realised His presence, His true nature through his experience is the knower of *Para-Brahma*; and he is not a *sanyasin* by outward appearance only.

(4) *Mahavakya Upnishad*

In this *Upnishad*, Brahmaji has exhorted gods about self-knowledge.

Brahmaji told the gods that only two reasons existed in the world for its bondage and salvation. They were ignorance and knowledge. One should understand it very well that this world is an eye (blind or closed) of ignorance. What you see with your eyes is not the truth. Only knowledge or wisdom guides and lights your path. The supreme knowledge is lit up by the light of *Brahma*. He is situated in your body in the form of soul and is always lit up. Treating yourself a part of Him, you should dedicate for long and realise your *pran*, *apan*, inhalation and exhalation. Then you will realise *Sachhidanand Paramatma* after having known his three different forms.

You should contemplate about all His forms because only then you would realise Him. There is no other path leading to salvation. One who repeats this realisation (of the knowledge of *Brahma*) in the morning is rid of the sins of night; and one who repeats this realisation in the evening is rid of the sins of the day. One should repeat this knowledge at noon time also with one's face towards the sun to free oneself from five serious sins (of eating meat, killing a *Brahmin*, drinking wine, gambling and having sex with the other's woman).

(5) *Atma Upnishad*

The form of *Paramatma* and the position of *Brahma* have been clarified in this *Upnishad*.

Paramatma is born in three forms – *atma* (soul), *antaratma* (inner soul), and *Paramatma* (the Supreme). In fact, nothing is real or true; neither ignorance nor knowledge, nor the truth of the world. All these things are *Brahma* only. Just as you know and accept the thing in front of you without asking for its proof in the same way with soul you do not need the proof of *Brahma*. In other words the knowledge of 'Soaham' is the direct evidence of *Brahma*.

Just as the sun is self-lit and lights the world, in the same way the whole creation of fixed and moving objects is lit up by the *tej* or light of *Brahma*. A person gifted with this knowledge is Rudra personified. He is free, emancipated in this life itself. Just as an acrobat comes back in his real human form after performing his acrobatic exercise, in the same way this soul, too, after leaving the body (on death) merges into *Brahma*. You just cannot imagine various attributes and faculties of that artless, actionless, quiet and peaceful *Brahma*. The truth is – *Brahma* is ncither born, nor unborn, neither bound nor aspirant, neither curious nor liberated. Nothing.

(6) *Gopal Purvatapniya Upnishad*

Shri Krishna has been described in a formless form in this *Upnishad*.

Once *Rishis* asked Brahmaji, "O Lord! Tell us who is the supreme God? who is it or whom death is afraid?"

Then Brahmaji said, "Shri Krishna is the supreme God? Death is afraid of Him. Once you know Krishna, dear to Gopis, you have attained all knowledge. *Svaha* (*Maya*) is driving the whole universe." The Rishis asked again, "Who are these – Govind, Gopi, Vallabh and Svaha?" Brahmaji replied again, "Govind is Shri Hari Himself—the destroyer of all sins, the protector and the knower of the *Vedas*, cows and the earth. He Himself is the *Maya*, and He Himself is the whole *Para Brahma*. In other words, he is the nurturer of the whole universe and pervades in everything. He is the *Brahma* and the whole universe of fixed and moving objects. He sustains His *Maya*. With the help of that power (*Maya*), He is the creator of this universe. *Kambeej* (*Kleem*) is the first part of the *mantra* of His worship. *Krishnaya, Govindaya* and *Gopijanvallabhaya* are the first, second and third parts of His *mantra*. One should worship Him with this *mantra* "*Kleem Krishnaya, Govindaya Gopijanvallabhaya Svaha*."

Brahmaji said further, "He inspired me to make this creation. From the 'k', 'l', 'ee', 'm', of 'kleem' *mantra*, I created water, earth, fire and moon, and from *kleem* created the sun. I created the sky and air from *Krishnaya*. I created men and women from *Gopijanvallabhaya*, and the universe from *Svaha*. This *mantra* leads to self-knowledge. In ancient times King Chandradhvaj attained self-knowledge with the help of this *mantra*."

(7) *Krishna Upnishad*

Shri Vishnu's incarnation as Shri Krishna has been described in this *Upnishad*.

Lord Shri Ram Chandra was the incarnation of the great Vishnu, in his *sachchidanand* form. When the forest dweller *munis* san Him they were both surprised and overjoyed. They expressed their desire to touch the body of Lord Shri Ram. On this Shri Ram said to them, "After this incarnation, I will again incarnate Myself as Krishna, then you, too, all will be born as Gopis and touch Me." So, all of them expressed their desire to be born as Gopis and cowherds. After that Shri Vishnu ordered all the gods to take birth as human beings but they did not agree to this saying that they were interested in living with Him and not in any birth. Then Shri Vishnu persuaded them saying, "I will live with you in the form of Krishna." Therefore, all of them became Gopis and cowherds.

The happiness and emancipation-bestowing part of the Lord was incarnated in the form of Nand and Yashoda. There are three forms of *Maya* – *Satvik, Rajasi* and *Tamasi*. The *Tamasi Maya* entered into the demons. It is very difficult to secure victory over this strange *Maya*, which is known as *Vaishnavi Maya* as well. In ancient times even Brahmaji could not overcome it. Gods go on worshipping it all the time. This *Vaishnavi Maya* appeared as *Devki*. The *Vedas*, which always worship the Lord, appeared as Vasudev. The meaning of the *Vedas* is Lord Vishnu. He incarnated Himself as Krishna and Balram.

This essence (meaning) of the *Vedas* appeared on the earth and indulged in various pleasure activities with *Gopas* and *Gopis*. The *Gopis* and cows of Lord Krishna are the *richas* (verses) of the *Vedas*. Brahma and Rudra incarnated themselves as the staff and flute of Lord Krishna. All the residents of *Gokul* were none others than the souls of those who were living in *Vaikunth*, the abode of gods and the Lord. *Tapasvi* people were born as trees there; and greed, anger, desire, other defects etc. were born as demons. All there vices in *kaliyug* are destroyed immediately on pronouncing the name of Lord Shri Krishna.

Lord Vishnu Himself assumed *Mayamaya* (illusory) body of *Gop*. This world is charmed and affected by *Maya*. As a consequence, it is very difficult to understand the *Maya* of the Lord. Even gods could not understand this *Maya* of the Lord. Because of this Maya Brahmaji incarnated himself as a staff and Rudra as a flute. Sheshnag was born as Balram, and eternal Brahma was born a Krishna. The sixteen thousand one hundred and eight queens of the Lord are the *richas* (verses) of the *Vedas* and *Upnishads*. Some other *richas* of the

Vedas were born as women of *Gokul*. In fact the demon Chanur is nothing but greed; likewise Mushtik is arrogance, Kuvalayapir is ego, and Vakasur, the demon which flies in the sky, is pride. Mother Rohini is mercy. The earth appeared as Satyabhama. Chronic diseases appeared as Aghasur and *Kaliyug* as Kans. Sham (restraint), truth and *dam* (control) appeared as Sudama, Akrur and Uddhav respectively. Conch is none other than Vishnu Himself. His conch, sounding like the clouds, was born out of *Ksheersagar*, the occan of milk. The flow of this *Ksheersagar* was the rivers of milk and curd which Lord Shri Krishna let flow by breaking pitchers. The Lord is indulging in various pleasure activities as He had been doing in His abode earlier. He is always busy in destroying the evil persons and protecting the saintly souls. The Lord assumed this human form for the protection of *dharma* and all living beings. The *Sudarshan Chakra*, equivalent to *Brahma*, the ultimate power, looks beautiful in His hands.

Air became the *Vaijayanti* garland round the neck of Lord Shri Krishna, and *dharma* itself became His soft *chanwar* (a device used to keep flies and mosquitoes away). Shivji assumed the shape of shining sword, Kashyap became the pestle in Nand's home, and mother Aditi became a rope. Decked and beautiful like vowels among letters, the sky overarching on all living beings became a canopy for the Lord. All those forms of gods in which the first poet Valmiki and Maharshi Vyas have described them and the forms in which human beings pay obeisance to them finally merge in Lord Shri Krishna.

Goddess Kali, always ready to destroy the enemies, became His club. Vaishnavi Maya transformed herself into His *Sharang* bow, and the life-taking death became His arrows. His hands look beautiful holding lotus, the seed of the destruction of the universe.

Garuda is Bhandirwat and Narad Sudama. The devotion itself appeared as Vrinda. The action-power of the Lord is the intellect which guides all human beings in knowing what their duty is. Therefore, all these *Gops* are not separate from God.

All the gods of heaven and *Vaikunth* were instrumental in the Lord's incarnation upon the earth. One who knows this secret enjoys the fruits of having visited all the places of pilgrimage is freed from the bonds of body; ie he is rid of the cycles of birth and death.

(8) *Ganapati Upnishad*

Ganapati, the lord of voice, has been described as *Brahma* in this *Upnishad*.

It is assumed that Ganapati lives in the *muladhar chakra* of human body. Ganapati represents all the four forms of voice (*para, pashyanti, vaikhari* and *madhyama*). He is *chinmaya* (conscious intelligence), full of happiness, and full of knowledge and science. He is beyond all the three *gunas* – solid, subtle and causal; and beyond all the three times – the present, the past and the future. He is Brahma, Vishnu, Rudra, Yam, Indra, *Agni, Vayu,* the sun, the moon, *Brahma, Bhuh, Bhuvah, Svah* and *Om.* The *mantra* of his worship is –

"*Nomo Vatpatye namo ganapataye namah
pramathpataye namastiastu.
Lambodarayaikdantaya vighnavinashine shiv sutaya
Shri varadmurtaye namo namah*|"

If you recite this *mantra* a thousand times then all your desires are fulfilled. One who coronets Ganapati reciting this mantra becomes a good speaker. By worshipping Ganeshji with this *mantra* along with shoots of *doob* (grass) a man becomes *Kuber,* rich like the god of wealth. Worship with a thousand *laddus* yields the fruits as desired. One who initiates eight *Brahmins* into the correct reading and recital of this *mantra* becomes bright and glowing like the sun.

(9) *Sharabh Upnishad*

The glory of Rudra has been described in this *Upnishad.* Once Rishi Pippaladi asked Brahmaji, "O Lord! Who among Brahma, Vishnu and Rudra deserves more consideration and contemplation?"

Brahmaji replied, "The body from which I am born is terrible Maheshwar Rudra. Even gods do not know Him due to their affection and ignorance. He is the decisive, discriminating intelligence of the *Vedas.* He is my father, as well as the father of Vishnu. In the end it is He who destroys this Creation. This Rudra, wearing skin as cloth, is famous with the names of Mahavir and Veerbhadra.

One should worship Lord Rudra for success in all activities. He is the destroyer. He killed death (time) with his left foot. He drank poison. When He was pleased, He gave the deadly *sudarshan chakra* to Shri Hari. It was He who had tied Vishnu in the snake-rope at the time of Daksha's *yajna*. His three eyes are – the Sun, the Moon, and fire. All the gods serve Him with awe as if they are animals. That is why He is called Pashupati. It was on His orders that Vishnu incarnated himself in many forms such a *matsya* (fish), *kurma* (tortoise), *varah* (pig) and Krishna etc. He reduced Kamdev (cupid) to ashes."

On hearing all this from Brahmaji, gods worshipped Him. Then Rudra freed gods from three kinds of sufferings – divine, bodily and physical, old age and death. He is the spark of the soul in all living beings.

A positive aspirant alone, free from any kind of dejection and doubt, can see that ever present *Brahma* with the grace of God. *Jeeva* is 'Shar' in whom the light of Lord Rudra is shining all the time. Therefore, He is *Sharabh Brahma*. He is the dispenser of emancipation. Beyond *para* is *Para-Brahma*, and beyond *Para-Brahma* is *Para-Rudra*. Therefore, one should continuously contemplate about Him, *Rudra*. One who knows all this is rid of sins and is emancipated in the end.

(10) *Devi Upnishad*

Various forms of *Maa Bhagawati*, in which she appears in the world, have been described in this *Upnishad*.

Once all the gods went to Bhagawati and asked her, "O Mahadevi! Who are you?" She replied, "I am *Brahma* in nature. I am the sole cause of origin of this world which in terms of attributes, has *Prakriti* and *Purush*. I am five *bhutas*; I am zero and non-zero, I am *Brahma*; I am the sky, the earth and the nether world; I am unborn, and the opposite of it; I move and flow in the form of *Rudras*, *Vasus* and *Adityas*. I am the water. I am the whole cosmos. The knower of this secret reaches my Lok."

The gods paid their respect to Her and worshipped Her.

We worship *Durga rup* (Goddess in the form of Durga) for eliminating our ignorance, Like Kamdhenu, she fulfils our wishes. She Herself is the destroyer of death; She is Vaishnavi, *skand mata* (the strength of Shiva), Saraswati, Aditi and the daughter of Daksha. She is *Tridev* (Brahma, Vishnu, Mahesh) and *Triguna* (*satva*, *rajas* and *tamas*). She is there in the form of all gods, planets, stars and time. Her basic *mantra* is 'Hrim', which fulfils all desires. The emancipatory *mantra* of Bhagawati is, "(Om) aim, hrim, chamundayai vichchai". This *mantra* bestows divine happiness, she removes difficulties. She is one, but pervades different, many forms.

Reading of this *Upnishad* in the morning destroys the sins of night; its evening reading destroys the sins of the day. Reading it both the times renders a man sinless. Its night reading bestows mastery over voice. If you recite it on a moonless night on Tuesday, you are spared the travails of death.

(11) *Sita Upnishad*

in this *Upnishad,* Sita is acknowledged in the form of Nature (*Prakriti*). 'She is the perennial power. She is *Yoga Maya.*' She has been described with this in mind. This *Upnishad* refers to and talks about twenty-one branches of the *Rig-Veda,* one hundred nine of the *Yajur-veda,* one thousand of the *Sam-veda* and five branches of the *Atharva-veda.*

Once gods asked Prajapati, "O Lord! Kindly tells us, who is this Mother Sita? What is her nature?"

On hearing this, Prajapati told them, "Sita is basic Nature. The word *Sita* is the name for three powers. '*S*' stands for *Satya* (truth), *Amrit* (nectar), *Soma* and indication of gain; '*Ta*' stands for extension and *lakshmirup* (wealth and opulence), and '*i*' means the *yogamaya* of '*Vishnu*', the cause of the entire universe. This *maya* expresses itself embellished with a lot of ornaments. When she is happy she bestows wisdom upon you. In her visible form she appears from the front tip of the plough of Janak. Her first form is *Brahma* in the word from. The form of '*i*', the third letter in the name, is invisible, unexpressed. Being always by the side of Shri Ram, '*Sita*' is the basis of the whole world. She is the root cause of origin and death of all living beings. The followers of Brahma call her '*Pranavrup mul prakriti*' – ie basic Nature comprising of Brahma, Vishnu and Mahesh, She is present in all living beings as conscious and unconscious soul. She is the base of all *Vedas,* *Loks,* gods and religions. As per Her attributes, She is in various forms such as gods, *Rishis*, men, *gandharvas*, demons and devils etc. She is stated to be (present in) five *bhutas*, senses, *mana, pran* etc.

She appears in the form of desire action and power incarnate. In the form of will power, she is effective, leads to welfare, *soma,* the sun and shows herself as fire. In her *Soma* form she produces medicines. She bestows the fruits of *yajna* on the gods. She bestows life on gods through nectar, and on human beings through food grains etc. She is inherent in the night, day, the light of the Sun, fire, food grains, medicines etc. She is located below the earth in the form of water as its base. Her form as an action power appeared from the mouth of Vishnu in the form of sound power. From sound to a point, from a point to *Omkar* and beyond *Omkar* is Ram – the Vaikhanas mountain. Many branches of knowledge and action emanate from Him.

The three *Vedas* are – the *Rig*, the *Yajur*, and the *Sam*. For successful achievement in action they have been given four names. The *Atharva-veda* is just another form of these three. It is acknowledged that the *Rig-veda* has 21 branches, the *Yajur-veda* has 109, the *Sam-veda* 1000 and the *Atharva-veda* has 5 branches. The first among these *Vedas* is the *Vaikhanas* opinion which is direct *darshan* (vision, philosophy). Therefore, the *Rishis* call it the best. The six *ang* (parts) of the Vedas are; *Kalpa*, *Vyakaran* (grammar), *shiksha* (instruction), *Nirukta*, *Jyotish* (astrology) and *chhanda* (stanza form). History. *Puranas Vastuveda*, *Dhanurveda* are called sub-*vedas*. *Varta* (discussion), *Dandaniti* (system of punishment) etc. are also self-revealed knowledge.

The voice (sound) of Vishnu appeared in the heart of Vaikhanas Rishi in the form of three *Vedas*. Vaikhanas has described it in the form of three *Vedas*. That is God's power, His obedience, She is the cause of birth, sustenance and death. The will power form of *Sita* is also of three kinds. She assumes the form of *bhog-shakti* (enjoying power) and at the time of deluge (destruction with inundating water). She rests at the right breast of the Lord in the form of *Shri Vatsa*. Later on, in the form of various power, such as the tree of desire, she rests in nine procedures. She gives birth to the articles of worship, places of pilgrimage etc. Her power as a brave person shows itself in a four-armed (form) appearance bearing lotus and bestowing boons. Gods such as Brahma stand around Her and worship Her with the *richas* of the *Vedas*. The sun and the moon shine near her as lamps. Worshipped by all the gods bearing a happy visage, she is brave Lakshmi, being the root cause of all actions.

(12) *Surya Upnishad*

In this *Upnishad* description centres round the oneness of *Brahma* and the sun in form and nature.

The *Rishi* of this *Upnishad* is *Brahma*; its god is Aditya (the sun) and its stanza form is *Gayatri*. His worship, too, is performed with the help of *Gaytri mantra.*

"Om Bhurbhuvah svah tatsaviturvarenyam
bhargo devasya dhimahi |
Dhiyo yo nah prachodayat | | "

i.e. He (the Sun) alone pervades *bhuh* (the earth), *bhuvah* (the cosmos), *svah* (the world of light). He is the Creator. We worship his *tej*, brightness and brilliance. He is used, is instrumental in all the four *purusharthas* (*Dharma, artha, kama, moksha*). The Sun god has four arms, he is the master of six (vowel) sounds, he sits ensconced on a six-petalled, seeded, red-colour lotus flower; having the glow and complexion of gold, he rides a chariot driven by seven horses. He holds lotuses in his two hands. One hand is raised in a posture of rendering all fearless, and the other hand looks like he is bestowing boons. A Brahmin who thorough knows the Sun God, handling and carrying forward the cycle of time, knows *Brahma* also.

His fame is worth choosing and singing. We contemplate Him. He should inspire and fire our minds. He is the soul of the whole world. All the loving beings, *yajna*, clouds, food grains and soul are born of Him. He helps you see and realise. He is Brahma, Vishnu, Rudra, *Yajush*, the *Sam* and the *Atharvaveda*, and all strange forms.

Everything is born of Him – all directions, air soil, water, light, gods and the *Vedas*. He is *Brahma*, the inner *soul;* five *pranas* and object of the senses of knowledge and action. Everything is born of Him and finally merges in Him. I am the same thing what the sun is. The sun is our eyes. He is everywhere.

'*Om*' has one, '*ghrinih*' has two, the sun has two and '*Aditya*' has three letters. They make the great *mantra* of eight syllables of the sun:

"Om ghrinih surya adityoma | "

One who reads and repeats this *Upnishad* daily realises *Brahma.* One should sit facing the sun and recite it to eliminate even chronic diseases. It removes poverty also. If you recite and repeat it in noon facing the sun, you are rid of the five deadly sins. One should never, nowhere praise this 'Savitri vidya', the knowledge of the sun. The Lucky ones who read it in the morning increase their good luck and fortunes, their cattle wealth and understand well the Vedas. If you read it all the three times (morning, noon and evening) you reap the fruits of performing hundreds of yajnas. If you read it when the sun is under hasta nakshatra effect of hasta star), you even conquer death.

(13) Prashna Upnishad

There are six questions raised by six Rishis in this Upnishad. Their separate answers are provided in dialogues, numbering six. Sukesha, Satyakam, Gargya, kanshalya Vaidasbhi and Kabandh were six Rishis who were well versed in the Vedas, were devoted to Brahma in his sagun (visible) form and were constantly in search of Para Brahma. Once they came to Rishi Pippaladi and respectfully asked him:

First Question: Kaband Rashi asked in all humility and faith: 'Who is that who is the supreme and definite cause of the birth of various jeevas of the fixed and moving universe?'

Answer : The Supreme (God) Himself performed tapa with a desire to create, and brought into existence the Sun and pran first of all. The Sun alone gives life and strength and the moon nurtures the solid (physical) body. The whole world is created with their combination. The name of the year is Prajapati (Parameshwar). The two parts of the year are – dakshinayan and uttarayan. Among them the name of dakshinayan is Ravi (Sun), and that of uttarayan pran. Those who worship with action orientation go by the dakshinayan path and reach Chandralok (the region of the moon). This is not permanent lok. After enjoying or suffering the fruits of action, jeeva has to come back to manushya lok, ie this earth. The wise persons take the uttarayan path and reach Aditya lok. They do not return from there.

Second Question: Bhargav Sukesha asked all three things together: (1) In all how many gods are there who assume (bear) the bodies (the pragya) of the living beings? (2) which one among them infuse or reveal it? (3) who is the best, noblest among them?

Answer: Maharshi Pippalad in reply said: This god, famous with the name of the sky, is in the nature of shelter of all the fixed and moving things. Air, fire, water and the earth are the gods and are born of him, and they are the cause of one another in a sequence. Air is born from the sky; then fire is born from air, water is born from fire; and finally the earth is born from water. In addition to them, eyes, ears and *mana* too are gods. The bodies of all living beings live under them. This *prani* (living being) assumes his body from these gods, therefore, they are the bearer gods. Voice (sound) and five senses of action, eyes, ears etc. the five senses of knowledge and *mana* etc. the four *antah-karan* – these fourteen gods are the bearers and revealers of this body.

Answering the third part of the question, the Rishi said that *pran* was the best of all. This *pran* is heated in the fire and the sun, which gives life to all. This *pran* alone is pervasive all over in the form of cloud, Indra and air. This *pran* is the earth and the Sun – it is the physical form of all living beings. Whatever is *sat* (truth) or *asat* (untruth) and *amrit* (nectar, non-dead) – all this is *pran* and nothing else.

Third Question: Ashvalayan asked with great humility, "Lord! From where is this *pran* born? How does it enter this body? How does it divide itself and how does it position itself? While leaving the body how does it go out of it? How does it bear the outside world? How does it carry on the inner conduct related to the soul?"

Answer: Maharshi Pippalad said that *pran* was born out of soul. Just as shadow of man depends upon man in the same way *pran* depends upon the soul. According to the desire of man at the time of his death *pran* enters the (desired) body. Just as there are many servants in attendance of a mighty king in the same way there are many like *apan* engaged in the protection of *pran*. In all there are five kinds of *pran* – *pran* resides in heart; *apan* resides in *guda* (sectum); *saman* resides in the navel; *dhyan* resides in the nerves; and *udan* resides in the nerves of *Sushumna*. So in this form these five *pranas* reside in the body. A man who has known and understood the mystery of *pran* never destroys it. *Pranas* reside in the semen, therefore it is very essential that one protects his semen in order to protect his *pran*. Observance of *brahmacharya* is the best remedy for protection of *pranas*. A person who while observing *brahmacharya* gains the knowledge of *Paramatma* who is the originator of *pranas*, gains immense and the highest happiness. So in this way a wise man who has known and mastered the entire mystery of *pran* is rid of the cycles of birth and death and becomes immortal and his progeny is never destroyed, mutilated or scattered. Tradition or family lineage continues.

Fourth Question: After this Sauryayani Rishi asked the following question: (1) who are the ones who sleep in this *purush* (man)? (2) who are the ones who are awake? (3) which god sees dreams in the state of dream? (4) who gains this happiness (happiness caused by sleep)? (5) In whom are these beings situated?

Answer: Maharshi Pippalad explained that just as all the says of the sun enter into it (the sun) at the time of setting in the same way at the time of sleep, a man neither hears nor seas, nor smells, nor tastes, nor touches, nor speaks, nor walks. In this way all his senses stop their work. Only *mana* is awake. *Pran* is also awake in the company of *mana*. The experience of dream is had by the *jeevatma*. *Jeevatma* experiences splendour and glory in the state of dream; later while seeing, hearing and experiencing, *Jeevatma* places the same scenes in the backdrop to compare with heaven.

When this jeevatma is overawed, overtaken by *tej* (glory and splendour), ie when *udan vayu* takes and places it in heart, the place of residence of *Brahma*, then it is surrounded by a kind of glow, and at that time all the senses including *mana* are (already) quiet; therefore, *jeevatma* does not see even the dream but experiences the rest (happiness) of sleep; because all are very well settled in *Paramatma* (at that time).

Fifth Question: Satyakam asked, 'Sir, suppose there is a man who has worshiped *Omkar* right upto the time of leaving his body. To which *lok* does he go because òf this (practice) action?'

Answer: In reply the Maharshi said, "Satyakam! This *Omkar* is definitely the *para* and *apar* form of *Brahma*. In other words, it is both subtle, abstract, faultless *Para-Brahma* as well as this visible world of the fixed and moving beings. This too is the total proof authority and existence of the same Brahma. Therefore, a wise man, a scholar who recognises and realises that *Omkar*, then he with the help and support of *Brahma*, gets/obtains *Brahma*, in *para* or *apar* form in which he desires Him.

After explaining the results of the three parts of *Aum* (*A+U+M*) the *Rishi* in the end says that the *Richas* of the *Rig-veda* make a man reach *manushya-lok* who devotes himself to one part (or *matras*) of *Aum*. The *mantras* of the *Yajur-veda* help a man reach heaven who has devoted himself to two parts (or *matras*) of *Aum*. The *shrutis* of the *Sam Veda* help a man reach *Brahma-lok* who has devoted himself to all the three parts (*matras*) of *Aum*. Only the wise know about this *Brahma-lok*. A man, who performs the *sadhana* of *Omkar* in a comprehensive manner, finally gets and realises the peaceful, undecaying, immortal, fearless, and the noblest and supreme *Paramatma*.

Sixth Question: Rishi Sukesha asked the *Maharshi* who that *Purush* (divine being) was who had all the sixteen *kalas* (arts).

Answer: The *Rishi* replied: 'O Sukesha! That *Purush* is here, he is inside this body of ours, in whom those sixteen arts reveal themselves. Elaborating the order of the origin of this creation, and coming to its conclusion the *Rishi* explained that the case of all things, the entire creation is like that of rivers. Rivers continue flowing with their face towards the ocean, and finally merge into it. On merger they lose their name and form both. They lose their separate independent existence, too. In the same way this entire cosmos, which has and displays all the sixteen arts, finally merger into its original storehouse: God. Then it has neither its name nor form. What remains in the end is only (and whole, comprehensive) Brahma. Since He collects back all his arts into Himself, He is artless and immortal / indestructible.

(14) *Mundak Upnishad*

This *Upnishad* is the best among all *Upnishads*, and is therefore treated as their forehead; and for this reason it gets the name *Mundak*. This *Upnishad* comes under the *mantra* portion of the *Shaunakiya* branch of the *Atharva-veda*. Two branches of knowledge, *para* and *apara*, have been described in it; the branch that leads you to the knowledge of *paramartha* (the supreme meaning sense) is *para vidya*; and the one dealing with the trends and tendencies of the worldly beings (*jeevan*) is called *apara vidya*. The first half of the *Upnishad* mostly relates to the *apara vidya* and the second half describes *para vidya*.

Shaunak Rishi asked Angira Rishi: "Tell me the element, the knowledge of which means the knowledge of all the (knowable) things."

In reply the Rishi said that the para and apara vidyas are the only things worth pursuing. The Vedas and the Vedangas are apara vidya. Para vidya is one that leads to the knowledge of Brahma. Paramatma is beyond the reach of the senses. He is all-pervasive, omnipresent. He is never destroyed. The wise persons see Him everywhere. That God alone is the root cause and substance of the whole world like the spider which creates its web from the substance in its stomach and finally takes it back into itself. God too creates the world and in the end takes it back into Himself. Trees, grass, food grains grow up on the earth in accordance with the seeds planted in it. In the same way, jeevan (pranis, living beings) assume their bodies depending upon the actions (good or bad) performed by them. And just as hair and nails on the body grow without any effort in the same way God does not have to make any effort of any kind in order to create the world.

The Upnishads say that Para-Brahma is highly, extremely shining and dazzling. He is light itself. He is more subtle than the most subtle object. All the loks and the living beings living in those Loks are actually living and located in Para Brahma. Para Brahma is the ultimate truth, immortal indestructible and the Last Word. The Upnishad tells you the way to reach, realise that Paramatma:

"Dhanurgrihitvaupanishadam mahastram.
sharvyupassanishitam sandhayit l
Ayamya tad bhavgaten chetasa lakshyam
tadivaksharam somya vididh l l
Pranavo dhanuhsharo hyatma brahma
tallakshyamuchyate l
Apramatten vedadhavyam shervattanmayo bhavet l l "

ie 'O Gentle Rishi! Take the bow as the strongest weapon, described in the Upnishad. Then place on it the sharpest arrow, sharpened by intense worship. Then stretch it long with your heart intently thinking of Brahma. And then aim and shoot (it at) Brahma placing your pure heart and soul into it. the sum and substance is that just as a brave hunter shoots an arrow on a deer, lion with great skill, and shoots it dead; in the same way an aspirant with all patience, practice, dispassion and soul – wisdom (keeping desires, affections, greed under control) should strike and pierce invincible object – *Brahma Pranav* is a bow, ie consider *Omkar* your bow. The soul, specially conscious mind / intellect is your arrow and *Brahma* (striking Him) is your aim. An alert, disciplined, unwavering man will strike (aim) Him. The one who is striking should become the arrow, as intent as the arrow, one with arrow, arrow itself.

Once a person realises Brahma, the cause and result of all (things) with efforts of this kind, then he has untied all the knots of *avidya* (ignorance) in his heart, and all his passions and desires disappear. All his doubts are dispelled and all the activities which impede the attainment of emancipation by an aspirant are weakened.

Explaining the subject further, the *Upnishad* says:

"Dva suparna sayugya sakhaya samanam vriksham parishasvajate |

Tayoranyah pippalam svadvattya nashnannanyo abhivakshiti | |

Samane vrikshe purusho nimagnoanishaya shochati muhyamanah |

Jushtam yada pastyatoyanyami shamasya mahimanamiti veetshokah | |"

In other words, *jeeva* and *Ishwar* are two birds, taking shelter of one tree. They always live together as friends and have a common history. One of them eats and enjoys the sweet fruits (of that tree) ie he anticipates the results of actions being ignorant, while the other does not eat or enjoy, it just goes on seeing everything as a witness.

In this way the ignorant *jeevatma*, though living with god on the same tree (body) yet due to his demeaned temperament is all the time getting affected, because he is finding himself unsuccessful in achieving the desired result and always fearing the unknown (impending) danger. But when he sees God and His labyrinth realised and untangled by the extraordinary *yogins* through their mertation, then he sheds his sorrow.

This statement means that on the body tree two birds, *jeeva* and *Ishwar* live together. Both have a common nature – *sat chit anand* (ie a true conscious and blissful nature). Of the two, the *jeeva* is entangled in the illusions and affections of the world and therefore suffers and enjoys the results of his actions. But the other stays quiet with a sense of detachment.

When the *jeevatma* is detached from the world, then it is liberated, emancipated.

How do you realise that soul (*Brahma*)?

The *Rishi* shows the way:

"*Nayamatma balheenen labhyo na cha*
pramadattapaso vapyalingat I
Etairupayairyatate yastu vidvanstasyaish
Atma vishate brahmadham I I"

In other words, a man can not realise this soul if he is weak, if he is lazy, or if he performs un-manly *tapasya*. You cannot live true *sanyas* with *yoga*-less *tapasya*. Only a faithful person committed to Brahma makes serious, sustained and sincere efforts, realises his soul, realises Him, inters into Him.

Therefore, a man has to wash sins from his heart, inner heart with the help of knowledge, truth *tapa* and *brahmacharya*. God can be revealed in a pure and cleansed heart only. One cannot know this God with the knowledge of classics (*shastras*) only. This *Upnishad* tells in all this in detail.

So we have seen that the *Upnishads* are an endless storehouse of knowledge. They inspire all living beings to be mutually sensitive and cordial. Man has himself been declared to be *Brahma* in the great sentence '*Aham Brahmasmi*'. Only *Brahma* himself can treat other persons as *Brahma* on equal level. Only the *Upnishad* can reveal and establish this feeling of equity, commonality. This is the reason why the *Upnishads* have been called the life-element of Indian culture. They endow the Indian culture with the title of being '*Arya Sanskriti*'.

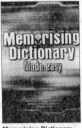

PERSONALITY DEVELOPMENT

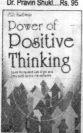

NEW PUBLICATIONS

Biswaroop Roy Chowdhury
Dynamic Memory Computer
Course (Updated & Revised)

Dr. Ujjwal Patni
Power Thinking

Namita Jain
How to Lose the last
5 Kilos

Tarun Engineer
Aim High For Bigger Win

Joginder Singh
Mind Positive Life Positive

Yaggya Dutt Sharma
The Lord of New Hopes
Akhilesh Yadav....

Ashu Dutt
Master the Stock Market

Ashu Dutt
Stop Losing Start Winning

Renu Saran
101 Hit Films of Indian Cinema

Renu Saran
History of Indian Cinema

O.P. Jha
Shirdi Sai Baba: Life Philosophy
and Devotion

Dr. Sunil Vaid
Why Does My Child Misbehave

Biswaroop Roy Chowdhury
India Book of Records

Biswaroop Roy Chowdhury
Heal Without Pill

Surya Sinha
Perfect Mantras For Succeeding
in Network Marketing

OSHO
The Osho Upanishad

OSHO
Sermons in Stones

OSHO
Tantric Transformation

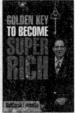
Subhash Lakhotia
Golden Key to Become
Super Rich

Subhash Lakhotia
Your Money My Advice

DIAMOND BOOKS X-30, Okhla Industrial Area, Phase II New Delhi-110020
Tel : 91+11-40712100, 40716600